CW01509634

THE INFINITE PLAYGROUND

THE INFINITE PLAYGROUND

PLAYGROUND

A Player's Guide to Imagination

BERNARD DE KOVEN
WITH HOLLY GRAMAZIO

EDITED BY CELIA PEARCE AND ERIC ZIMMERMAN

The MIT Press
Cambridge, Massachusetts
London, England

This book was set in Adobe Garamond and Berthold Akzidenz Grotesk by Jen Jackowitz. Printed and bound in the United States of America.

Library of Congress Cataloging-in-Publication Data

Names: DeKoven, Bernie, 1941-2018, author. | Gramazio, Holly, author. | Pearce, Celia, editor. | Zimmerman, Eric, 1969- editor.
Title: The infinite playground : a player's guide to imagination / Bernard De Koven with Holly Gramazio ; edited by Celia Pearce and Eric Zimmerman.
Description: Cambridge, Massachusetts : The MIT Press, [2020] | Includes bibliographical references.
Identifiers: LCCN 2019043534 | ISBN 9780262044073 (hardcover)
Subjects: LCSH: Games. | Games--Social aspects. | Play. | Imagination.
Classification: LCC GV1201 .D373 2020 | DDC 793--dc23
LC record available at https://lccn.loc.gov/2019043534

10   9   8   7   6   5   4   3   2   1

Contents

BEGINNING BEFORE THE BEGINNING *xi*

Foreword: Press Play *xi*
  Celia Pearce

Introduction: Editing Bernie *xvi*
  Holly Gramazio

What-if-ing *xix*
  Rocky De Koven

INTRODUCTORY *1*

Pre-posthumous *1*

The University of Imagination *5*

Something to Play: *Prui* *7*

Imagining a New World *11*
  Jesper Juul

Every Now and Then *12*
  Lee Rush

A Million Ways to Play with Bernie, at Least *14*
  Gonzalo Frasca

THE FUNDAMENTALS OF PLAY   *17*

Something to Play: *Reception Line*   *17*

Occupy Fun   *19*

Occupy Play   *21*

Something to Play: *J'Accuse*   *23*

The Well-Played Game   *25*

Having Fun Together   *28*

Something to Play: *Tag*   *30*

Changing the Game   *31*

When Can We Play?   *33*

Getting People Playing   *35*

Something to Play: *Eclipse*   *36*

After You've Played   *38*

Imagination and Possibility   *39*

Something to Play: *Sound Travel*   *41*

Compassion for the Play of Others   *43*
  Sebastian Quack

A Lifetime of Play   *45*
  Frank Lantz

Girls Own This Playground   *48*
  Katie Salen Tekinbaş

THE PRIVATE IMAGINATION   *51*

Strengthening the Imagination   *51*

Something to Play: *Silly You and Serious You*   *52*

Something to Play: Walking Games   *55*

Failure of the Imagination   *57*

Something to Play: *Blather*   *59*

Flowing with Imagination   *61*

Something to Play: *Making Faces*   *63*

The Imagined Audience   *64*

Something to Play: *The Orchestra and the Conductor*   *67*

Slow Play   *70*
   Tracy Fullerton
Ever Since   *73*
   Adriaan de Jongh
Roll with It   *74*
   Greg Trefry

THE SHARED IMAGINATION   *77*
Something to Play: *Darkroom*   *78*
The Collective Imagination   *80*
Coliberation   *82*
Something to Play: *Group Blather*   *87*
Of Me and We   *89*
Something to Play: *Signifying Nothing*   *92*
Risking Coliberation   *95*
Something to Play: *Moving Pictures for the Community Theater*   *97*
Encouraging Coliberation   *99*
Something to Play: *Zen Counting*   *101*
Something to Play: *Handland*   *102*

Tilt-Mate   *104*
   Ian Bogost
Focus on the Fun   *106*
   Zack Wood
Play Sets Us Free!   *108*
   Stephen Conway
Come Out & Play   *110*
   Catherine Herdlick

THE WORKING IMAGINATION   *113*
Something to Play: *Singing Blather*   *114*
Daydreams and Doodles   *115*
Something to Play: *Drawing Together*   *116*

Imagination and Creativity   *118*

Making Imagination Real   *119*

Something to Play: *Foley a Capella*   *122*

Imagination and Science   *123*

Strengthening the Group Imagination   *126*

Why Imagine?   *127*

Something to Play: *The Label Game*   *129*

Play, Imagination, and Business   *131*

Something to Play: *The Orchestra Game*   *133*

Enter the Dragon   *136*
  Mary Flanagan
Coliberation   *139*
  Douglas Wilson
Like Many of My Generation   *141*
  Akira Thompson

BEING IN THE WORLD   *143*

Imagination's Role in Creating the World   *143*

Something to Play: *The Blather Chorale*   *145*

The Ecological Imagination   *147*

Something to Play: *Ways of Bee-ing*   *148*

The Compassionate Imagination   *150*

Something to Play: *There Must Be a Good Reason*   *153*

The Moral Imagination   *154*

Having Fun Together   *157*

Something to Play: *Passing Humanity*   *158*

Imagination and Endings   *160*

We, the Prui . . .   *163*
  Colleen Macklin
Stepping Aside   *165*
  John Sharp

A Lightening   *166*

  Tassos Stevens

A LACK OF CONCLUSION   *169*

Quitting Is Heavenly   *172*

  Elyon De Koven

Afterword   *174*

  Eric Zimmerman

FURTHER READING   *177*

CONTRIBUTORS   *183*

Beginning Before the Beginning

FOREWORD: PRESS PLAY

CELIA PEARCE

Have you ever played with a giant rainbow parachute with your kindergarten classmates, carefully positioned yourself in a giant circle of playmates to sit on one another's laps, or tried to untangle a giant human knot as part of a teambuilding exercise? If you've done any of these things, then you've experienced the world—and the imagination—of Bernie "Blue" De Koven.

Bernie De Koven, always ahead of the curve, devoted his life to studying, designing, writing, and teaching play and playfulness. In the late 1960s and early 1970s, he developed a play-based elementary school curriculum in Philadelphia. In the early 1970s, he built one of the first archival game collections, known as the Games Preserve, decades before game studies existed as a discipline. As president of the New Games Foundation in the mid-1970s, he was instrumental in the spread of games like the ones described above—many of which became ubiquitous—to such disparate contexts as nursery schools, summer camps, theater courses, and corporate offices. He also had a hand in designing a number of his own games. Although his oeuvre was decidedly analog, in 1982 he designed *Alien Garden*—released by Epix for Atari and Commodore 64 and programmed by VR pioneer Jaron Lanier—a game that is largely viewed by game historians as the first digital artgame. He designed games for and with clients such as Mattel, Ideal, LEGO, and the Children's Television Workshop. At the same time, he was involved in several scholarly communities, including the Association for the Study of Play (TASP) and the North American Simulation and Gaming Association (NASAGA).

Not Too Cool for School

Bernie's work was originally introduced to the nascent videogame studies community in 2003 through Katie Salen Tekinbaş and Eric Zimmerman's *Rules of Play: Game Design Fundamentals*, which liberally referenced his 1978 book *The Well-Played Game: A Player's Philosophy*. The desire to find our roots, to discover who had come before us, led Katie and Eric to introduce his ideas to a new generation engaged in thinking about play from not only a practical but also a theoretical perspective. Bernie conjoined these two approaches seamlessly. His ideas about games, though informed by theory and scholarship, were the result of a lifetime devotion to active engagement with play.

My first encounter with Bernie was in 2004 when he gave a talk and series of workshops hosted by Tracy Fullerton and Janine Fron at the University of Southern California (USC). Bernie's presentation, which focused on his concept of "coliberation," was a revelation to me. Immediately after his talk, I approached him and asked, "Will you be my guru?" He laughed and replied, "Will there be money involved?," to which I replied,

"No, but there will be citations." Bernie's ideas about the "play community" became so foundational to my PhD research that I titled the resulting book *Communities of Play*.

I have a vivid recollection of my first experience actually *playing* with Bernie, around the same period, on the lawn in front of USC's Annenberg Center, along with Janine, Tracy, and Jacki Morie, with whom I would later go on to form the women's game collective Ludica. For me, the experience was transcendent. Even though I had relished in physical play and make believe as a young girl, competitive sports had traumatized me, and it was emancipating to think *Was the game good enough for the players?*, rather than the other way around. Bernie's work was central to Ludica's philosophy. Our paper "Sustainable Play: Towards a New Games Movement," published in the journal *Games & Culture* in 2007, called for a revival of the movement he had a hand in starting, complete with its anti-establishment agenda. There were a handful of contemporary practitioners we cited, some of whom are among the contributors to this book. Even as we were writing, the nascent "new New Games movement" was already underway in the form of events such as Come Out & Play in New York and Hide&Seek's Sandpit in London—with which Holly Gramazio was intimately involved.

Bernie also influenced IndieCade, prompting myself and my cofounders Stephanie Barish and Sam Roberts to embrace "new New Games" as part of our purview. For IndieCade 2012, he gave a keynote conversation with Eric Zimmerman, and led us in a Junkyard Golf workshop based on his 2005 book *Junkyard Sports*.

Although he was already influential in game studies by 2011, many game scholars (including a number of contributors to this book) had their first encounter with Bernie himself at the Digital Games Research Association (DiGRA) conference that year. Initially, some were taken aback by his simple message of embodied play. Weren't we trying to get people to take games seriously? Wasn't all this touchy-feely silliness just a throwback to the '60s? Skeptical at first, they stepped into Bernie's particular brand of "Magic Circle" to get a different perspective on games as both a cultural *and* a social practice. Games were not just about *analyzing artifacts* and *rules*. They were also about *experiencing play*. Bernie's appearance coincided with what might be termed the "play turn" in game studies where, increasingly, researchers were expanding their attention from games as systems of rules and cultural artifacts to lived player experience. Many of these people were also instructors who integrated Bernie's ideas about embodied play into their pedagogical methods. His play session at DiGRA 2011 was a who's who of game scholars, many of whom are contributors to this book.

Infinite Play

I got word of Bernie's diagnosis in late March of 2017, while in Los Angeles dealing with the sudden illness and death of my stepmother. He had put out a call on social media asking for help on some remaining projects he wanted to finish. I immediately contacted him to find out how I could help. The first matter at hand was this book. Eric Zimmerman had also reached out to him and was able to secure a contract with the MIT Press, but the book needed a coauthor with the time to take on the dedicated writing role.

We talked about a few options, and I recommended Holly Gramazio. I first met Holly at Come Out & Play, where I had seen her give a masterful talk about play in cities. Holly was one of the members of Hide&Seek, the UK-based game design collective and producer of big games events in London, and I had worked with her in several contexts, including as the jury co-chair of IndieCade. She struck me as the ideal person for the job. When I ran into Holly a month later at IndieCade East in New York, I flat out asked her if she would do it. She happily agreed to sign on to the project.

In this book, Holly has exercised a phenomenal sleight of hand that few could have mastered. When she received Bernie's original manuscript, the basic ingredients were there, but it needed some major reorganization and rethinking. She worked very closely with Bernie to craft its organization, and also to curate the contributors. The result is a textual conversation that weaves gracefully between Bernie's philosophical musings; various games that he learned, designed, or taught; and commentary by a wide range of scholars and practitioners whose work he has influenced.

The small essays in this volume provide just a sample of many "magic circles" with which Bernie has intersected, from game makers, to game scholars, to curators and festival founders (myself from IndieCade, Sebastian Quack from PlayPublik, and of course Holly from Hide&Seek), and to teachers, who are keeping Bernie's work alive by passing it on to their students. This is important since the vast majority of his games are performative; we don't have many "artifacts" associated with them.

More than anything, this book is a conversation—between you, Bernie, and an all-star cast of game designers and scholars, moderated by its amazing coauthor, Holly Gramazio, and Eric Zimmerman and myself. There is no doubt that Bernie's work lives on through the writing of others, such as *Rules of Play*, Tracy Fullerton's *Game Design Workshop*, and so on. His spirit also lives on through IndieCade's "Bernie DeKoven Big Fun Award," which was introduced in 2017, shortly before his death the following year.

On a grander scale, Bernie's philosophy seems poignantly timely, not only in the broader field of play, but in society writ large. Rather than play a zero-sum game, we can imagine a different type of play with the goal of mutually benefiting each other, whether through competition, cooperation, or both. In this sense, Bernie's message is intensely relevant to the present moment and we would do well to heed his call to "play well with others" and imagine together not only a better world, but a better us.

INTRODUCTION: EDITING BERNIE

HOLLY GRAMAZIO

I never knew Bernie well. I knew his work, of course, his books and his games, but Bernie himself? Only a little.

I started making playful work around 2007, with a strong focus on games in the physical world. My philosophy of play was very different from Bernie's—I was interested in play as a communicative medium, something to use for my own ends rather than an end in itself—but it was still exhilarating to come across *The Well-Played Game* and other documents from the New Games movement, and to be able to situate this "new" work that we were making within this wider context.

As my involvement in play and game design deepened, I would run into Bernie occasionally. We presented games at a few of the same festivals, chatted briefly a couple of times, exchanged a few emails. It felt important to see someone who'd been working in play for decades, and who'd approached it in so many ways: as an archivist, a designer of both physical and digital work, a curator, a writer, a facilitator, and always as a player. Even now there aren't many models around of what it means to spend a life thinking deeply about games, about how to make them and teach them and play them. I felt Bernie's occasional presence, and his blog, his talks, his writing, and his ongoing practice, as something that showed it was possible.

And then he sent me a manuscript for his new book. This book. Even now, this is the main way I know him: through reading and rereading and reconfiguring, trying to find the best arrangement of the many different sections and fragments of possibility.

He'd written a few drafts of the book when he decided to hand it over to concentrate on his treatment and his family and friends. Each draft came at the same core ideas in a different way, using different examples, arrangements of games, and overarching frameworks. But the heart of the book was there each time, of course: the idea of imagination as a playground to which we have almost infinite access and the concept of learning how to imagine as a way of learning how to live.

We spoke to Bernie a lot throughout the early months of the editing process, making sure we understood his intent with the work, and thinking about the various ways we could approach it and arrange the different ideas. He sent over related blog posts as well, and interviews he'd given: anything that was an articulation of his last five years or so of thinking about the interaction of imagination and play, in whatever form.

Our intent with this book was to thread together these diverse thoughts and approaches and turn them into the best articulation we could assemble of the ideas that sat at the heart of his numerous drafts. Sometimes this meant pulling examples and games from his online writing, or removing suggestions and ways to play that were wonderful but muddied the main direction of the work. Sometimes it meant writing the titles of dozens of different games on index cards and sticking them up on a mirror and moving them around and around until they fell into place. Sometimes it meant reading one of the essays from our many contributors and understanding something new about how one of the games Bernie had written played out in practice. Sometimes it just meant reading over a passage for the third or fifth or tenth time and suddenly seeing it with fresh eyes, understanding as if for the first time its purpose, framing, and sidelong jokes, and finally seeing how the whole chapter could fall into place.

Bernie died before we finished our revisions, but we'd talked with him about his message and his words a lot, and about structural changes and how we were planning to put things together. It's been an extraordinary set of thoughts, suggestions, and ideas in which to spend so much time; I hope we've managed to do them justice.

WHAT-IF-ING

ROCKY DE KOVEN

"What-if-ing." So much creative, even scientific, work plays with the What If.

What if I use this color, that chord, this movement, those words, that ingredient? Can I surprise myself?

The product is (almost) secondary to the process—what you go through as you plunge into the uncertainty.

Try it. What could possibly go wrong? Oops!, or Wow! Then try something else.

Imagine that!

INTRODUCTORY

PRE-POSTHUMOUS

As I write this chapter of the book (after, of course, I've written everything else), I am slowly accepting and resisting the meaning of "palliative care." I'm not too worried about this because it's pretty clear which, acceptance or resistance, will prove the correct response.

And as I write, I'm imagining you reading this, or maybe having it read to you, or both. And I imagine you as a playful soul, always open to the possibility of an even bigger playground, and even more amazing things to play with.

And have I got some good news for you!

Those most infinite of all playgrounds, and the most infinite of playthings, are those of imagination itself. Imaginary playgrounds. Imaginary playthings.

As I wrote this book, I decided to imagine you. And then I wrote this whole thing as if it were written only for you, my imagined you. And from time to time, I imagined us writing it together.

Really. Together.

Maybe as you read this book, you could imagine me reading it to you. Not in my voice, but in yours. (Imagine I'm very good with voices.)

Maybe we could pretend that there is no difference, no distance between what you read and what I write. And that as I find words for things, you are also finding words for them. You assemble these words together, imagine them into being, make them make sense, vision, sound. You give them voice. Your voice, maybe.

So, really, we are the writers of this book. As you read it, you write it. It becomes yours. You put the words together into a vision. And it becomes your book, too.

And as the writers of this book, I think we should build marvels of fun in our imaginary playgrounds—so marvelous and so marvelously powerful that, though they don't rely on any tool or object or anything we think of as "real," they can become part of reality; they can change reality.

It is in these infinite playgrounds, in the very nature of infinite playthings—in the things we make up, pretend, imagine—that we play with the powers of the soul. We can pretend that we, ourselves, are infinite, both individually and collectively, infinitely.

Because, as you know so well, we playful beings have a lot of different playgrounds. Give us a bunch of marbles, packaged or pretend, and we create a marble-ous playground where everything is a target or a ramp or a tunnel—something to roll over or under or through or into. Give us an imaginary whistle (I mean the best imaginary whistle we can imagine) and everything is about how long and how loud and how many different ways we can make it sound. Better yet, give everybody a whistle. And an imaginary playground for sound (every, any sound), played on the ultimate instrument of our imaginary voice.

Every toy, by its very toyness, is a door to yet another playground. We grown-ups call these playgrounds "hobbies." We professional grown-ups call them work. We whittle. We carve. We sculpt. And each opens its own world that exists for us only as long as we keep whittling and carving, blowing and rolling, working and making. As soon as we stop playing, as we must eventually do, the play becomes finite, formed, fixed, a "work."

All these playgrounds, even the one this book is in, involve what we call "imagination."

Imagination is an infinite playground.

Imagination grows by exercise, and contrary to common belief, is more powerful in the mature than in the young.

—SOMERSET MAUGHAM, *The Summing Up* (1938)

The power of imagination makes us infinite.

—JOHN MUIR, *John of the Mountains:*
The Unpublished Journals of John Muir (1938)

THE UNIVERSITY OF IMAGINATION

And so here you are at the Imaginary University. Welcome.

The Imaginary University is, precisely as you may have surmised, imaginary. It exists only in our individual and collective imaginations, and is neither more nor less than you or I imagine it to be.

The College of Playful Learning of the Imaginary University is, as all colleges within the imaginary campus are, also imaginary.

This project, the Infinite Playground project, invites people in the fields of game design, film, multimedia, science, art, architecture, and literature to join in a collective effort to create new, and concurrently imaginary, invitations to playful learning so that students and professionals might explore and exercise their imagination.

Such an endeavor cannot be successfully achieved by offering courses in how to be more imaginative, as such courses carry with them the very disincentives to imagination that have caused the problem in the first place. Joyless exercises in "strengthening" the imagination are self-defeating because it is not one's imagination that needs to be strengthened but one's opportunity to recall and experience once again the joy that imagination can bring.

I, Bernard Louis De Koven, aka Blue, imaginary dean, have spent more than fifty years writing and teaching innovative approaches to games, play, and the imagination. This is what, through the College of Playful Learning, I hope to bring to you: a play-centered invitation to experience the power and delight that your own imagination can bring to you and to the imagined universe.

There are many justifications for helping people—especially designers, inventors, and innovators—exercise and develop their skills in using their imagination. But it is the imagination as a play thing, an entertainment and gateway to wonder and pure play, that is the main focus of this curriculum. The theory being that by bringing attention to the fun of it, the rest will follow.

The curriculum is intended to function primarily as a professional tool. It is a demonstration of playful learning. The games can be shared in class and communities, inside but especially outside of the academic environment. Though the theoretical component provides background, it is included more as an incentive than as a study guide. Secondary disciplines for this curriculum focus on creatives (artists, writers) and people who work with people who spend a lot of time by themselves (home bound, bed bound, incarcerated, elders . . .).

As part of this curriculum, sitting alongside the games and techniques and observations I've gathered over my many decades of play, I'll also be quoting some of the game makers, scientists, writers, thinkers, and imaginers that have influenced me.

I hope they might influence you, as well.

This book, or course, or course book (of course), is divided into five main chapters:

The **Fundamentals of Play** is about games, and the way games and play can give us access to the gift of imagination.

The **Private Imagination** is about playing inside our own heads, and what it means to imagine on our own.

The Shared Imagination is about the wonders that can happen if we start imagining together—and some things I've learned over many years on how to coax that experience into existence.

The Working Imagination looks more explicitly at imagination as a professional tool—at the way artists and scientists and even businesses have used imagination to make things, and to make things happen.

And finally, **Being in the World** talks about how our imagination can connect us to everything around us—to each other, to nature, and to the wider world.

Throughout the book, I've included invitations to **play** and **imagine**—rules for games, exercises, and ways that you might want to use your imagination, or encourage other people to use theirs, or both. The rules are just suggestions, of course. Feel free to change them. But I've tried to tell you a little bit about what makes each game or exercise interesting, and how it might make you feel, and what it can help you to do and see and imagine.

So before we get into the chapters of the book we've just talked about, let's have a look at one of my favorite games, just to get started.

SOMETHING TO PLAY: *PRUI*

Clear the dance floor (living room, kitchen, backyard). Get more or less everyone together. (Only the people who want to play. For any game to be fun, participation has to be optional.)

When the mass is about as critical as it will get, begin the game by asking everyone to close their eyes and start milling around. The milling should be, as all proper milling is, aimless and random and, insofar as this is eyes-closed milling, slow and sensitive.

When two milling people bump into each other, they should shake hands, while one of them says "prui." If the person they encounter says "prui" back, they each go off to find someone else. On the other hand (as it were), when someone bumps into the actual, pre-appointed Prui, shakes hands, and says "prui," the Prui shakes hands, doesn't say anything, and doesn't let go. Now both people are Prui, and they remain Prui until the end of the game. If either of them is encountered by anyone else, more people are added to the Prui.

The game continues until more or less everyone has become Prui. Then they can open their eyes. There are some exceptionally fun moments as more and more people feel their way toward Pruiness. The game gets quieter and quieter while the plaintive sounds of the unPruied few saying "prui" become more and more distinct as they seek contact with the ever more scarce welcoming hand.

I think I might have made this game up. I thought I read about it in a book about games from many cultures, in the section about games from Holland. I have since not been able to find that book. And when I visited Holland, I couldn't find anyone who had heard of the game. I eventually taught it at a New Games Tournament; it was then described in *The New Games Book*, disseminated to the alternative-fun-seeking world, and remains one of my favorite walking-around games. In fact, it has become such a favorite that I have noted in myself a marked propensity for launching into dramatic narrative about the significance of the Prui and general Pruidom.

For example, the significance of having your eyes closed.

You could have blindfolds for everyone. Then you and everyone would be conceptually assured that you would all be equally in the dark, the shared darkness being a significant factor in making this game as fun as it is. I, on the other hand, prefer to ask people simply to close their eyes.

Closing your eyes means that you have access to something I like to call "minimal cheating." Since people are walking around with their eyes closed they feel somewhat at risk, exposed, as it were, threatened, perhaps. I suggest, therefore, that if people feel uncomfortable enough, they open and close their eyes, very, very briefly, camera-shutter-like. It's cheating. But if it's done quickly enough, it's minimal and doesn't distract from the various joys of blind milling.

Or take the significance of bumping into people, in a big chain of Prui, all holding hands.

Here again some minimal cheating might be advocated. After all, you are walking around with your eyes closed. And if you're part of the Prui, holding hands with two different people, you have nothing to protect yourself from the inadvertent grope or bump. Thus, you might feel the need to absent yourself from Pruiness for a moment or two and open your eyes. By all means, do so. But endeavor ever so sincerely to do so briefly—very, very briefly.

Further, once people are found, and are within the links of Prui, they often find themselves sorely tempted to open their eyes for longer than one would consider a minimal moment. Thus I frequently find myself commenting on how the longer everyone can keep their eyes closed, the more fun it is when the game is over. This isn't a game with a winner, of course. It's a game about fun and being together. And so everyone who is playing—or else they wouldn't be playing—wants to make it fun.

This reminds me: frequently, people ask me, "how do you know if you are the Prui?" This is a most reasonable query. I respond thusly: "I, as leader pro tem, will either whisper into someone's ear something like 'you are the Prui,' or wait until a self-appointed Prui emerges."

Sometimes, this results in the spontaneous generation of two or several Prui-groups. Which, though you might not think so at the time, seeing as it blatantly desecrates the unspoken hope that all will ultimately find themselves part of one undivided Prui, nevertheless results in a gregarious gathering of group glee.

As you can see, these exercises aren't just for telling you about some games, but are also for discussing why those games work and how they work. After all, if you're reading this then there's a good chance that if you ever play *Prui*, you'll be the one explaining it to everyone, summoning the play and the imagination, whispering "you are the Prui" into someone's ear to begin.

So sometimes when we talk about a game or an exercise— since this is, after all, a university, albeit an imaginary one— I'd like for you to think about what it might be like to play, how you might go about explaining the game to others and encouraging them to play, and whether there are any changes you would make. And I'll try to share everything I've learned about these games through all my years of trying them out and inventing and reinventing and imagining and playing.

IMAGINING A NEW WORLD

JESPER JUUL

Bernie De Koven was adamant that you didn't have to play with him. It was just that you always really wanted to, and that playing with him felt like tapping into a source of pure primordial magic. Bernie would introduce a game with a smile, and everything would come alive. What you actually *do* in a game of Bernie's is simple, but it feels like being part of a grandiose scheme, a real-yet-imagined world where the simplest action carries immense weight and meaning, but you perform it with ease, and you feel that you must start laughing.

I spend much of my time analyzing games, but with Bernie it felt like skipping the design phase and going straight for the feeling of being in instant lockstep with something that goes beyond being just a system of rules: when playing *Prui*, you walk around with closed eyes, shaking hands with everyone you meet, until you suddenly meet someone who *is* Prui, and you yourself become Prui, and then all players are Prui. You begin worried by the prospect of becoming Prui, but in the end it is deeply comforting, as if you have been saved and can finally relax. You never learn what "prui" means.

Bernie's games are fun because they are so serious: relating to social anxieties; being or not being part of a group; learning new languages with secret meanings; taking off your shoes; the intensity of rational planning followed by a breakdown of plans; being caught; all the people with their guarded faces becoming one.

If Bernie was a "master of ceremonies," it was nevertheless his central point that control should be shared; we should all make and change games. It was his hope that in this way we might learn not to take rules, systems, or social orders for granted. By learning to play and change games, we learn to create change outside the game.

Our task, then, is to have more imagination. To pretend that we are someone or something else, to see a twig like an animal, to see ourselves as something new, to imagine our social group as working in a new way, to imagine that the people we have just met are lifelong friends. When we play with Bernie, it is not just that we imagine things to be different than they are; we also imagine how they could be different. Yet the value of play is also intrinsic: through play and imagination we can lead fuller and more magical lives.

EVERY NOW AND THEN
LEE RUSH

Every now and then a seemingly insignificant event happens in life that is never, ever forgotten. At times, the happening may be nothing out of the ordinary; it could be just another day or another conversation with a friend or a complete stranger. And then again, a single conversation can make an indelible mark on one's life. And this is exactly what happened to me when I met Bernard (aka Bernie/Blue) De Koven way back in July of 1979. It was during a week-long New Games camp held near Philadelphia. I was a young, not-so-sure-of-myself twenty-four-year-old among a group of older, seemingly more established others in the professional world of educators, counselors, and recreational leaders.

During our time together at camp, we played games, learned about group dynamics and game design, and kept hearing about a planned trip to a place called the Games Preserve. I had no idea what a "games preserve" was, but I do remember the excitement when the leaders talked about spending time with the custodian and owner of the preserve—Bernie. I recalled reading Bernie's well-known essay in *The New Games Book* called "Creating the Play Community."

And so we went. If you have never been to a games preserve, imagine this: a lovely country farm with a century-old house and barn filled with every game you could think of, and more. There was a climbing rope for those so inclined, board games if you pleased, a pool table, parachutes and other supplies for creating new games, and of course there was Bernie and his family. I recall spending much of the day there, having lunch and more conversation, and then it was time to leave and say goodbye when it happened. I turned to say farewell to Bernie when he said, "It's been great meeting and playing with you. I'll tell you something, too—I really like you and like your energy! Keep coming around." That was it. A simple expression of gratitude. As I said, maybe it was because of my age or mood that day, but when Bernie simply shared his heartfelt thanks and joy in meeting me, it seemed I had just been knighted by King Arthur himself. I was filled with wonder at what he may have seen in me that I did not even notice myself.

I went on to become a teacher and counselor at an alternative school. I became a serious student of play and used games to build a "play community" in our school. I stayed in touch with Bernie and had him come and speak at a youth conference I planned later in my career. To me, Bernie was a friend, mentor, and, perhaps most of all, a teacher and an example of living in the moment and saying what is on your mind. Because all we have are moments, they come and go . . . and before you know it there are no more.

One of Bernie's favorite games was *Prui*, and I was honored to lead the game at the Day of Play Festival put on in Bernie's name shortly after his passing. *Prui* is one of my favorite games that I learned from him. You get to hide (if you are the Prui) and to seek the Prui (if you are not it). Better to play the game than explain it!

Anyway, I can only imagine Bernie getting up to the pearly gates and when greeted by St. Peter, the only words he says are simply: "At long last—PRUI!"

A MILLION WAYS TO PLAY WITH BERNIE, AT LEAST
GONZALO FRASCA

There's a short text, an appendix to Bernie De Koven's *The Well-Played Game: A Player's Philosophy*, about marbles. It's a playful text that flows like a playground conversation.

I like to assign it to my game design students, but only after asking them to teach me how to play marbles. Usually my students will teach me a couple of variants that they learned as kids, none too different from the way I used to play in my schoolyard with Samantha Navarro, who was feared and respected by all her peers for her uncanny superpower when it came to throwing tiny spheres.

Once my students agree on the most standard rules, we read the appendix together, discovering the marble big bang that Bernie imagines: marbles made with ice, with water balloons, with steel, going through mazes and pipelines and ending up inside cups. We don't even have to hold marbles in our hands to visualize the possibilities: galaxies of possible marbles orbiting inside our imagination.

Together we realize that the text is not about marbles. Actually, that not even the game of marbles is about marbles. It's simply just an excuse for playing, negotiating, discovering, and experimenting.

That's how you play with Bernie, even if you've never personally met him. You walk into his work thinking it's all about games and play and only then you realize—as he teaches you—that it's about people clumsily discovering their own humanity.

THE FUNDAMENTALS OF PLAY

This is a book about imagination.

But it's also a book about games. A book about play. A book about really playing in the real world, and a book about imagining what it might be like to play in the real world, and a book about how play and fun and imagination can change how we feel—about each other, about the world, about ourselves.

Imagination and play are not quite the same thing. But they're not quite different things either. And play is one of the best ways I know to imagine. So let's start there: by playing. In fact, let's play a game right now—or, at least, let's imagine we're playing a game.

This game is called *Reception Line*, and it's about introducing yourself, so it seems like a good place to begin.

SOMETHING TO PLAY: *RECEPTION LINE*

Get a group of players together.

Mill around.

Decide who you are. You could be anybody, really, with any title or none, with any name or none, mighty or mighty strange, from ancient parentage or unknown origins. You might even decide, or help others to decide, your purpose for being here. A celebration? An award ceremony? A chance to meet the first lady? A funeral, perhaps?

Find someone. Introduce yourselves—whoever you may be at the moment.

You are now a couple. Embrace each other. If you wish to continue your conversation with your newly found other, pray do so. If not, wait until you are approached by another couple. Assume the "reception position"—standing side by side.

Each couple introduces itself and/or each other to each member of the new couple. Each participant is free, of course, to redefine themselves. After everyone in both couples has exchanged introductions, you become a foursome. Decide, if you are collectively moved, on a collective identity, a hidden agenda, and so on, until you decide that the time has come to be an eightsome. You'll need to find another foursome, and all introduce yourselves, each to each.

As an eightsome, you continue until you are greeted by another committee of eight. Each eightsome assumes the reception position once again, and on with the introductions.

You might, for the fun of it, introduce a certain formality to the reception process, shaking hands or bowing or curtseying to the next person in line, who introduces herself in greeting with a salutary and otherwise kind manner. Formality, or something reminiscent of formality, becomes the rule. When Ms. Alice has sufficiently introduced herself, she goes down to the next person in line; the person she just greeted (the Honorable George) waits politely until Ms. Alice has introduced herself to the next person in line (Dr. Spark) and then follows her, introducing himself to Dr. Spark.

Or, for the fun of it, decide that it's a wedding reception and, instead of all that bowing formality, spend the time hugging and being hugged by bride and groom and family members.

The reception continues until the two largest possible communities have formed, or until everyone has had the opportunity to introduce themselves to everyone else at least twice. There is no reason for this.

Did you play? Probably you didn't: probably you don't have sixteen or thirty-two or sixty-four friends or friendly strangers with you, waiting to join in a game. That's okay. But do me a favor. Imagine that you played, just for a minute. Imagine what name you might have chosen, how you might have introduced yourself, what secret motive you might have picked. Imagine what you might have said to your partner, and how you might have introduced your partner to the couple you joined to make a foursome.

OCCUPY FUN

Now that we've played a game, or imagined that we've played a game, we can think about exactly what that means.

To connect to the play mind, it helps to build a vocabulary that we can use to evoke that state of play purposefully—a vocabulary that is vivid enough, clear enough, and acceptable enough to us that we can at least pretend it into being.

Let's start with "fun."

When we were children, we had fun, like children. When we grew up, we pretty much stopped having fun.

Well, we didn't exactly stop having fun. But we convinced ourselves that fun wasn't a grown-up reason to do things—not really a justification, certainly not something to be proud of.

So whatever it is we did for fun became, in like manner, something we didn't have a good excuse for. Having fun, playing games, pretending, daydreaming—not what we'd call mature, not what we'd think of as grown-up.

"Fun" became a three-letter four-letter word. Something we don't talk about in public. Something we don't even talk about much in private.

So here's the idea:

Occupy fun.

Occupy, as in engage, as in connect with, as in make it ours, as in appropriate, celebrate, bandy about, talk about, use a lot. Use it to describe the things we like to do, to ourselves, for ourselves. Treat fun as reason enough in itself. Find out what there is about our relationships, our purpose, that we can honestly and totally call fun. Find those memories, those moments that we can truly call fun. If it doesn't feel right, find the parts, the implications, the nuances that do.

Could we call eating ice cream fun? Kissing someone we love? Meeting people we know—people who are as glad to see us as we are to see them? How about giving money to someone who needs it? Listening to someone who needs to be heard? Comforting someone in pain?

Let's see what it's like to use the word—even if it's just to ourselves—as honestly and as often as we can until it has meaning again, until it is totally and clearly ours. Not the same meaning, perhaps, that it had when we were children. But the mature, adult, practical, enlightened meaning for the person we've become.

OCCUPY PLAY

If we can be comfortable again with fun, how about play?

In case you hadn't noticed, you really like to play. Whether you play in public or not, whether you play games or not, whether you have toys or not—you like to play.

I'm writing this to you because I can imagine, given all the stuff about play you'll be finding in this book, and how more and more people seem to be writing about play, offering workshops, seminars, lectures, classes in play, even, how it might make you wonder about yourself, make you ask yourself: "do I play?," or "do I play enough?"

It's a good question to ask yourself. A useful thing for you to think about. But don't kid yourself. You play. You were born to play. When you see an animal or child or even an adult at play, you respond playfully.

Imagine a dog, sitting down with a ball in front of it, looking up at you with its big dog eyes.

What is that dog doing?

Inviting you to play, yes, no?

How'd you know? What made you so sure? Okay, the ball was a clue. But you know dogs. They were born to play. And you know it because you know play when you see it, because you play. You have always played.

Sure, you could play more. All you need is the opportunity, the permission—and both of those (opportunity, permission) are things you can give yourself.

It's a choice, this being in play, and to make this choice you need to be aware that such a gift is available to you and yours, all the time.

To play you don't need toys or costumes or joke books. You don't even need games, although they can help. But you do have to be open, vulnerable. You do have to let go.

Play is all about that vulnerability, about being responsive, yielding to the moment. You might not be playing, but if you are willing to play, at the drop of a hat, the bounce of a ball, the glance of a toddler, the wag of a tail—then you are open to any opportunity. You are loose. Responsive. Present.

Play means presence, but not just presence. Responsiveness, but not just responsiveness. Presence and responsiveness, lightness and attentiveness, improvisation and creativity, a willingness to let go and become part of something new.

Play is one of the signs scientists look for when trying to determine the health of a herd of animals. The healthier the animals and the safer the herd, the more they play.

The same is true of the human herd. Especially herds of children. As long as the kids are healthy and feeling safe, left to their own resources, play is the thing they do.

Adults of the herd play less, at least observably, perhaps because in many cases they are not as healthy or as safe as they were when they were children.

But adult human beings are different than the adults of any other species I can think of, in that they can choose to play, even when they don't feel safe or particularly good.

And when they are at play, they tend to feel healthier, safer, almost like they might have when they were kids, and maybe even better. And even though they are fully conscious adults and even though they can't ignore the danger, the consequences, the very real lack of safety that is threatening their entire health forever, they can choose to be at play. And they can reclaim for a moment their health, their well-being, the energy they might have had in their youth—simply by playing again.

SOMETHING TO PLAY: *J'ACCUSE*

J'Accuse is a detective game for those who like their mysteries fraught with hilarity. It's about dying.

Dying isn't fun. Being dead, in all likelihood, is not fun. Someone else's death, even a pet's death, is not fun. And yet, and yet playing dead is immensely fun.

When we're young, we pretend to die in games. Playground games and videogames and more. Clutching the imaginary arrow as it penetrates your core, falling back into the arms of your fellow knights, foamingly swooning into momentary oblivions. And how about all those shoot-'em-up computer games where the only way to figure anything out is by getting killed by something.

And we grow up, and still we need to play with death. Like anything else we need to understand, especially when it comes to big, hurting things that are too vast, too painful to grasp, death and dying are things we need to play with. Over and over again. Not only because we need to understand them, but because it's the only way we can even begin to accept them as real.

It's odd. We don't really know what it feels like to die. But we imagine. We can pretend. And therein lies the fun.

To play *J'Accuse* you need at least, oh, seven people. Ideally I like to play it with maybe twenty-five.

Everyone starts the game milling around. Shaking hands randomly. Engaging in idle conversation. While the whole lot of handshaking is going on, the referee (or whatever you want to call the person who's teaching the game) selects someone to be the murderer. This is accomplished by means of a secret hand-shake known as the "palm tickle."

The murderer commits the heinous crime by means of a similarly secret, but this time *poisonous*, palm tickle. It's a slow-acting poison, and the dying are encouraged to delay their death throes by at least several seconds. Of course, the dying are fur-ther encouraged to engage themselves in the full range of con-tortions and gasps normally accompanying death by drama.

If at any point you—while still alive, of course—think you know who the killer is, you shout "J'Accuse!" You don't actu-ally do anything at this point. Everyone immediately refrains from any further handshaking and milling. According to the rules, nothing happens until someone else says the equivalent of "J'Accuse, too." In other words, an accusation is not a true accusation unless it is seconded.

At that time, both the first and the second accusers point at the accused. If they point to the same person, that person must reveal his or her true identity. If they point to someone who is not the true murderer, or if they point to different people, they are both dead, and entitled to die as horrible a death as they deem advisable. If the first is not seconded, he or she too must die.

And so the ever more fortunate and dwindling few meander into the depths of feigned fear and frank frolic, while the dead play smugly dead . . . until the murderer is brought to justice or there are only three left among the living.

The person who was murderer the last round selects the murderer for the next, in much the same manner.

THE WELL-PLAYED GAME

J'Accuse is a marvelous game for groups, and for getting everyone involved (everyone who wants to play, naturally), and for being as silly as you want to be. It's a marvelous game to get people feeling comfortable with each other, and finding their way into a playful space.

It's a game I've been playing, off and on, for a very long time now.

Forty years ago I wrote a book called *The Well-Played Game*. In the book, I explored the core experience that makes games worth playing, and the politics that surround making that experience accessible.

The best way I can introduce you to the book is with a story about myself and my friend, Bill Russell (who was, not coincidentally, a professional player). It was during the time we were still building the Games Preserve.

There we were, up in the barn, playing with our brand new, thoroughly researched, ultimate ping-pong table. That barn was the center of what we were calling the Games Preserve. We wanted to fill it with not only every game on the planet, but the very finest manifestation of each. And Bill chose that particular table, and those particular paddles and balls, and installed some very particular kind of lighting for precisely that reason. It was not just a ping-pong table. It was *the* ping-pong table.

Bill knew that I couldn't really play ping-pong. And I knew that he could really, really play. And because we wanted to play together, we just more or less volleyed (he more, me less). After a while, Bill suggested that I just try to hold my paddle still enough that he could get the ball to hit it. Apparently, that was more than challenge enough for the both of us—for him, hitting my erratically moving paddle so that the ball would bounce off in exactly the right angle, with precisely the correct speed. For me, figuring out how to move my body while simultaneously holding my paddle in a position something similar to perpendicular. Every time the ball actually crossed the net, hit my paddle, and got back to Bill was sheer magic for me. After a while, we managed to get an actual volley going, Bill exercising the depth and fullness of his ping-pong skills, me magically holding my paddle where it needed to be. And after a longer while, we got a very, very long volley going. And during that volley, the ball seemed to take on its own, almost internal light, as if it were inhabited by our spirits, Bill and mine, combined. And it was, for an instant, as if we were seeing God. Honest. When we left the barn, it was like we had just achieved enlightenment. It was a moment when the actual and imagined coincided, blended into an experience of the whole.

That one single experience led me to writing what I still believe to be the most important book of my career.

Bill and I had shared something inarguably powerful, deeply transforming, but not quite tangible. Something that seemed to me to be the real reason for the Games Preserve, the real reason that games are as important, as worthy of deep study and exploration and investigation as I felt them to be. Something so important that winning and losing were incidental, games' mere artifacts: trophies, trinkets.

Game-wise, Bill was far better at ping-pong than I. But play-wise, we were equal. And Bill knew that he could use his skills on our mutual behalf, trying to get the ball to hit my paddle so that we could come together in play.

It was an experience of mutual transcendence—of going beyond skill, beyond personal limits, beyond the very boundaries of self. The experience of being part of a well-played game, of what I eventually named "coliberation." (Remember that word, if you like. We'll talk more about coliberation later.)

If it hadn't been for Bill's expertise and compassion, and for our mutual willingness to find a way to play that allowed both of us to play together, at our best, I would never have reached the understanding of what being part of a well-played game was all about. It's the kind of experience that's normally accessible only to the finest athletes (and only rarely), and to children who are young enough not to know better.

One of the best descriptions I've encountered of this experience—of playing a game that makes us feel more than ourselves—is something Bill wrote in his book *Second Wind: The Memoirs of an Opinionated Man*. I thought this might be a good passage to share with you, to help get across what I'm talking about. (Of course, he's not talking about ping-pong here. Bill Russell might be a ping-pong champion but he's also one of basketball's all-time greats.)

> Every so often a Celtic game would heat up so that it became more than a physical or even mental game, and would be magical. That feeling is difficult to describe, and I certainly never talked about it when I was playing. When it happened I could feel my play rise to a new level. It came rarely, and would last anywhere from five minutes to a whole quarter or more. Three or four plays

were not enough to get it going. It would surround not only me and the other Celtics but also the players on the other team, and even the referees. To me, the key was that both teams had to be playing at their peaks, and they had to be competitive. The Celtics could not do it alone.

You should really read the whole thing:

> At that special level all sorts of odd things happened. The game would be in a white heat of competition, and yet somehow I wouldn't feel competitive—which is a miracle in itself. I'd be putting out the maximum effort, straining, coughing up parts of my lungs as we ran, and yet I never felt the pain. The game would move so quickly that every fake, cut and pass would be surprising, and yet nothing could surprise me. Even before the other team brought the ball in bounds, I could feel it so keenly that I'd want to shout to my teammates, "It's coming there!"—except that I knew everything would change if it did. My premonitions would be consistently correct, and I always felt then that I not only knew all the Celtics by heart but also all the opposing players, and they knew me. There have been many times in my career when I felt moved or joyful, but these were the moments when I had chills pulsing up and down my spine.

It was an experience like this, my own experience with Bill, that made me think about what it means to play well, and that in turn made me want to write *The Well-Played Game*.

HAVING FUN TOGETHER

Of all the things that contribute to accessing the experience of the well-played game, none has more influence than the community of players, or, as I prefer to call it, the "play community." I prefer to call it that because it helps me make a clear (and what I have found to be a very useful) distinction between that and the "sports community."

In the sports community, the rules and officials decide if the players are good enough to play. If not, players are exchanged. So, to reach the point that Bill Russell talks about in the previous section, the players need to have mastered the game to such a degree that they can reach beyond not only their personal limits, and their collective limits, but also the limits of the game.

But in the play community, we—the players—can decide if the game is good enough to play. If not, we can change the rules. The ultimate criterion for success is not so much who wins, but much more: how much fun we are able to create for each other. In this way, every game is continually being designed by the play community.

And the thing about fun-focused games is that they're not so much about the fun that any one particular player or team is having. Usually, no matter what game you play, somebody has fun. The thing that makes this whole idea so worth thinking about is that fun-focused games are all about everybody having fun, certainly everybody who wants to be having fun.

This kind of game, the fun-focused kind, is not about getting the highest score, even though points might be awarded and scores might be kept. Getting the highest score is not the point. Winning isn't the point. The point is getting to share that special state of spirit, mind, and body that we call "fun." And maybe we can experience that special feeling that I had in that shed with Bill—without anyone having to be a world-class athlete.

In fact, let's do that now. Let's play another game—or, at least, imagine that we're playing another game. And let's make it something we all know, so we can think about how we might change the game, and let other players change it, too.

SOMETHING TO PLAY: *TAG*

We all know tag. Or at least, we all know one version of tag.

Depending on which version of tag you're playing (and they are legion, these tag versions), you either want to be IT, or you don't want to be IT.

When you're IT, and you don't want to be IT, you have to make someone else be IT, and the only way you can do that is by, eponymously, tagging someone.

And then you're not IT, and someone else is, so you run away.

So the question, then, is: "If tag is a game (which it certainly is) then how do you win?"

And the answer?

Well, it seems you don't really, quite exactly, win. The game just goes on and on. You're either one of the many, running away from IT, or IT, running after the many.

Sure, when you're IT you can go after one or several people in particular, for whatever reason you can give yourself: revenge, friendship, vindication. And if you manage to tag them, it's almost like winning. Except, when you succeed, all that happens is that person becomes IT, and they get their turn at revenge, or a demonstration of friendship, or whatever. You still don't win. And neither do they. And when you're not IT you can look at every moment of your not-IT-ness as a personal victory. But, sooner or later, you'll be caught. And if you're not, it's almost like you lose, because the only real object of the game is the fun you have playing, and, after a while, being not IT is just not fun enough.

If being IT is winning, then why are you trying so hard to make someone else IT? If being not-IT is losing, then why are you running away?

Because it's fun.

And if it's not fun enough then you can make it fun. Whenever we play tag we have to agree on what the rules are because there are so many different ways to play, and that means we have to make up what the rules are. We change them. We make a version of the game just for us, for where we are and who we are and how we feel. Maybe if IT doesn't stay IT long enough, we make rules like "no tagging back." Or, if people are getting too tired or not tired enough, we change the size of the play area, or we declare certain places "off limits" or "safe" or "home." We're not making a new game. It's still tag. But we're fine-tuning it because it's ours, because it's for fun.

CHANGING THE GAME

Being able to do this—to change the game—helps to create that sense of glorious play together. If something isn't working, you can try something a little bit different.

There are many strategies for designing a game as it is being played. One is most often called "cheating." There are degrees of cheating. If we judge the effectiveness of cheating in terms of fun, then the most effective kind of cheating is when the cheater actually makes the game more fun for all the players. In *The*

Well-Played Game I call this "the well-timed cheat" because it is usually put into practice at the moment it is most needed—just when the game isn't as much fun as it should be, when people are getting too serious about winning or losing, when they are at risk of getting hurt physically or emotionally. So somebody does something that not only is a flagrant violation of the rules, but also makes everyone laugh. Like knocks the pieces off the board, or runs out of the game and comes back with two more balls, or starts a song that leads to a whole new game.

If you remember *Prui*, the game we talked about in the introduction, then you'll find a great example of a well-timed cheat that makes the game better: sneaking a look through your not-quite-closed eyes. It can be just enough to help you feel safe and confident as a player, enough to make the game more fun for everyone.

Sometimes, the easiest way to bring a game back, and the players back, and reach something wonderful, is to take a break. This is called quitting. And quitting works best when everyone does it at the same time. But sometimes, all you need is one person to quit—because by quitting, that one person reminds everyone that quitting is possible, that the game itself is something that is being played only because everyone wants to play it. It's only a game, and the only reason it's being played is because it's fun, or supposed to be. And if it's not, well, we can just quit and play a different game or make up a new one entirely.

On the other hand, making up an entirely new game is not so easy. It's a lot easier to take an old game and change it—a rule or two, or something else.

To start, maybe try something from this list of "Seven Ways to Make Almost Anything More Fun," which I compiled with suggestions from Matt Weinstein, Elyon De Koven, and Jon Jenkins.

1. If there are two sides, add a third or take one away.
2. Every now and then, change sides: when someone is ahead by two somethings or when someone throws a 9, or when somebody has to go to the bathroom.
3. If there are turns (checkers, gin rummy, serving the ball in ping pong or volleyball), take them together, at the same time, as in "1, 2, 3 . . . go," or every now and then skip a turn.
4. If there is score, keep playing until you discover who's the second winner, and the third, and the next, and the last. Or give each other points, or play pointlessly.
5. If it's not fun, change it: add another ball, or a rule, or a goal, or take a rule away, or change a rule, or borrow a rule from another game, or add a whole game and play them both at once, or do something playful.
6. If it's still not fun, change yourself: try it with your eyes closed, or with your "wrong" hand, or tie yourself to someone else.
7. If it makes the game better, for everybody, cheat.

These aren't the only ways to change the game, of course! And the people playing a game will be the best people to work out what would make it more fun for them—if they feel comfortable enough to try.

WHEN CAN WE PLAY?

Another thing I talk about in *The Well-Played Game* that is important for the sort of play we're talking about now is the feelings people need to have in order to really be able to play, in order to be able to reach the sort of transcendent experience that play can become.

First, safety.

We need, in order to be willing to be willing, some guarantee, somewhere, that no matter what happens in our pursuit of the well-played game, we will not be risking more than we are prepared to risk. Even though I'm aware that I might die as a result of trying to climb this mountain with you, I can accept that as part of the game. On the other hand, when I discover that the game allows you to cut my rope so that you can get to the top first, I find myself much less willing to play.

So, even though this willingness thing seems to be a prerequisite for our discovery of the well-played game, willingness, pure and simple, isn't enough. We need to feel safe within the game we want to play well together.

Then, trust.

The safer we feel in the game we're playing, the more willing we are to play it. But, for this experience of safety, we can't rely solely on the game. We must also be able to believe that we are safe with each other.

And familiarity.

In order to trust each other at all, we need to establish some basis of familiarity. If we haven't played with each other before, we are not familiar enough to be sure of each other.

If we are playing a game that we are all familiar with, chances are that through playing the game together we will be able to establish some minimal basis of trust.

As we play with different people, we discover that there are variations of the games we have become familiar with. If we are familiar enough with our game, and if we are really interested in sharing play with others, then we can play a variation without losing the sense of safety that familiarity provides. On the other hand, there are hundreds of games and tens of variations for each—more than we could ever hope to become truly familiar with.

This is where a deeper understanding and a deeper set of conventions about play come in.

If we can understand and standardize certain aspects of all the games we play, we will extend our basis for familiarity. Rules such as taking turns, playing fair, playing the game through to the end, and good sportsmanship are all conventions—derivations from different episodes of play, general rules that allow us to arrive at an ever-broader standardization.

Violating a convention usually results in a stiffer penalty than violating any particular rule of a game. By establishing the intention to play well together we have begun to create a new convention. We would like it to be understood that the search for the well-played game is what has brought us together. We would like to make this agreement clear enough between us that we can assume it to be inviolable.

GETTING PEOPLE PLAYING

Almost any social/physical game—any game that invites us to play together with each other—also invites the imagination.

But some games seem to invite us to be exceptionally close and most definitely imaginative. They shift the way we see each other, understand each other. They redefine us from individuals to collectives and back to individuals. They're funny, they break down barriers, they invite us to see each other, and ourselves, differently. They are physical but only mildly so, so the focus is more on the social play than on the physical. But they are physical enough to help us get into and out of our bodies, to identify with how we see each other and how we are seen by each other.

I've been asking you to imagine that you're playing all sorts of games, but I haven't talked about how you might get to that point of playing. How, if you do have a group of friends with you who want to play, you might help them to feel safe, how you can help to establish conventions, how you can choose to play and imagine together.

So this time I'd like you to imagine not just that you're playing a game, but that you're telling a group of other people how to play. Maybe imagine that you're reading the rules from this book to them, or that you've remembered the rules—you think you've remembered the rules—and you're telling everyone as best you can from memory. And the game I'd like you to imagine explaining is called *Eclipse*.

SOMETHING TO PLAY: *ECLIPSE*

This is a game with lots of walking around. Walking-around games are especially attractive when playing with larger groups, as a case in point of the more-the-merrier condition.

This one is based on a game I found in a book called *Games for Actors and Non-Actors* by Augusto Boal. He called it *Eclipse*, so we might as well call it that, too.

We begin the game with everyone walking around aimlessly. Sauntering, so to speak, from pillar to post, from hither to thither or yon. At some time, some self-appointed leader-like person (perhaps imagine it's you) says "find your sun," meaning that everyone should imagine that one person in the group is their own personal sun. Of course, this fact is never divulged to one's personal sun. It is merely decided on internally and then acted on externally. From that time until the game is over, the goal is to stay in the sunshine. Since everyone, including everyone's imaginary sun, is still generally milling, while everyone is now trying to stay within his or her own personal sunshine, there is ample incentive for even more pervasively general milling.

The leader-like person then suggests that the general millers include a moon in their imaginary solar system. Again, everyone selects their imaginary moon, again internally without outward sign or verbal divulgement. For the rest of the game, the goal becomes to stay within one's personal ecliptic—positioning oneself so that one's personal moon is between oneself and one's chosen sun.

Now, because we have what some astronomers call the "three-body problem," millers find themselves milling ever more rapidly. Their sun is moving. Their moon is moving. And they are moving, nay, scurrying, perhaps even running amuck, trying ever so diligently to keep their appointed moon between themselves and their selected sun until the purported leader says "freeze."

Then, in somewhat amazed breathlessness, everyone points to their moon with one hand and their sun with another, and those who find themselves uncannily positioned so that their moon is between themselves and their sun can consider themselves "winners."

They could, you know, lie. I mean, no one really knows who chose whom to be what. But, because there is no point in winning, there is similarly no point in lying. Which is, as a matter of fact, a great relief for all.

Nor is there any particular significance in being someone's chosen sun or, for that matter, moon. Yet, as the game progresses, the collective imagination becomes so wonderfully vivid that surprisingly merry interplanetary mayhem unavoidably ensues.

Did you imagine explaining the game, and then playing it? Even if you didn't, I'll imagine that you did.

AFTER YOU'VE PLAYED

What happens after you play a game? You've created a world together—what next?

If you find yourself in a position where you're helping other people to play, then one of the most powerful things you can do is invite them to stop between games and talk and think and rest; let them reflect on their play and become impatient to play again. Sit down, if you like. Talk about what you did. What was a moment that was funny? What did you notice? What might happen if you changed the rules a little more?

Sure, once you've gotten people playing a game together, you could just rush into another game. But if you want people to end up feeling comfortable with each other, inventing and reinventing, suggesting different ways to play, imagining new games into existence—then after playing, just take some time to think and talk.

Perhaps just ten minutes. Schedule it in, and make sure that your participants are able to share pretty much anything that comes to their mind, whether it was prompted by their experience of the game or not.

Each of these ten-minute interludes can follow the pattern established through play: there is no such thing as a wrong response, and each response incorporates the responses of the players who spoke before.

For example, after the earlier game in this chapter, *Reception Line*, the first player might say something like: "As soon as I was part of a group larger than four, there was never enough time for us to introduce everyone to everyone else." The next player: "The larger the group, the more we seemed to laugh." The next: "And as the game continued, we got sillier and sillier with our selection of identities." It doesn't matter so much what people say—just that they have time to say it.

When people are impatient to play, you can move on. And again, it almost doesn't matter what you play. Just that you do. And that you do it together.

IMAGINATION AND POSSIBILITY

You may have heard of, or even read, James Carse's famous *Finite and Infinite Games*. Less well known than its title is its subtitle: *A Vision of Life as Play and Possibility*. The subtitle hints at a profound postscript to an already profound book: life as play and possibility.

Our imagination brings us close to something like pure possibility. We can imagine, or at least pretend, anything. Literally anything. As we move from imagination to creativity, we, of necessity, begin to limit the possibilities we are ready to consider. It's like moving from just playing around to playing a game, or from doodling to making art. Once embracing infinity, we seek the finite.

We do this because it is more rewarding, more fun. We get to make something out of the world and ourselves. On the other hand, the creative act depends just as much on our ability to move back into play. This ability to move back and forth between the finite and infinite is what we call "playfulness."

To understand the nature of imagination, we must explore the interaction between imagination and possibility. Fortunately, we will find insights into that interaction in the writings of Alexander Manu and his *The Imagination Challenge*. It's probably best for me to use Manu's own words, and the words of the other philosophers and scientists that he's responding to. So let's imagine a conversation between all the parties in question, shall we? Manu quotes the philosopher and cognitive scientist Nigel J. T. Thomas:

> Imagination is what makes our sensory experience meaningful, enabling us to interpret and make sense of it, whether from a conventional perspective or from a fresh, original, and individual one. It is what makes perception more than the mere physical stimulation of sense organs. It also produces mental imagery, visual and otherwise, which is what makes it possible for us to think outside the confines of our present perceptual reality, to consider memories of the past and possibilities for the future, and to weigh alternatives against one another. Thus, imagination makes possible all our thinking about what is, what has been, and, perhaps most important, what might be.

Manu's response to this powerful idea builds on it further, bringing more philosophers into the conversation:

> Nothing we imagine is absolutely impossible, according to Scottish philosopher David Hume. Once we have the capability to

form images in our mind, we can define the capabilities needed to bring these images to life—to enable them as technologies. Based on our experience of the world around us, our imagination constructs only images of possibility. If something seems impossible, it may also be unimaginable.

Manu talks about two different types of imagination: one that reconstructs the past, and one that restructures and extends our experiences. It is this second type of imagination that creates: "creative imagination is credited as the basis of all human achievement in the sciences and in art," he says.

We create through imagination. And once again, we can imagine—if we want to—through play.

SOMETHING TO PLAY: *SOUND TRAVEL*

Some games are so mellow, so laid back, that people are prone, so to speak, to take short naps while playing. Not that they are bored, but rather, shall we say, transported.

Sound Travel is just like that. Players lie down or sit around, usually with their eyes closed. All they do for the rest of the game is make noises.

Before the game starts, one player suggests a theme. Here are some examples:

A day in the life of:

- an iron worker
- a teacher
- a parent
- a baby
- a puppy

- a crocodile
- a meteoroid

Some others: A trip to Rio. The evolution of man. An earthquake. A moon landing. Armageddon.

Once the vocal majority, or someone, has agreed on a theme, the journey begins. Players simply start making noises with their mouths and accessible body parts. These are, supposedly, the sounds of the journey as they travel through the location, or event, or experience, or time.

There's no point or purpose. The goal is to somehow agree on where and when you are, and all end together. And therein lies the fun.

COMPASSION FOR THE PLAY OF OTHERS

SEBASTIAN QUACK

When I first encountered Bernie De Koven in 2014, he was teaching a workshop at w00t festival in Copenhagen. People were doing something silly with their hands. There was laughter and joy. I didn't get it. "Looks like they're releasing their inner child," I remarked to a friend.

At the time, I didn't know much about Bernie's work apart from images of New Games events, people playing with a huge ball . . . it seemed very 1970s. I had spent the last several years in Berlin trying to establish public play as a contemporary art form, running festivals, writing applications. In retrospect, I was being a Really Serious German about play.

I didn't think more about it, but I kept getting recommendations for Bernie's book *A Playful Path*. When I finally sat down to read it, I came across the following passage:

> As adults, given the opportunity, finding the permission to come out and play together—we can bring all those years of power, experience, compassion, all those competencies and strengths, all the stories and histories, all our sophistication and post-pubescent powers into play. We can release the inner-adult.

I was confused—was this the same guy? I was intrigued, and felt ashamed of my earlier dismissal. Here was a line of thinking describing beautifully how being playful—especially when it might look childish (or juvenile, or in any other way different) from the outside—can be a deliberate, adult, political act.

My second encounter with Bernie was after running the Playpublik festival in Kraków. As we talked on Skype about the pleasures and pitfalls of inviting adults to play, I was amazed at Bernie's curiosity about the specifics of how and why other people play.

When Bernie told me the story of how an accident during *Earth Ball* resulted in a lawsuit that spelled the end of the New Games Foundation, we talked about the fragility of communities of play and the risks involved in facilitating unconventional ways of playing.

At Playpublik, there had been not only a game with a similar big ball bouncing through the city, but a multi-kilometer hopscotch across as many property lines as possible, and a Russian-style scavenger hunt with real cars, fog, and dangerously abandoned sites. We were lucky there had been no accidents or lawsuits.

Since then, I've continued to work with adult play, compassion, risk, and responsibility, and Bernie's thinking about releasing "the inner-adult" has stayed with me.

One area where this has been especially fruitful is Playful Commons, a project about permitting everyone to play. It's similar to the Creative Commons licensing model that allows the sharing and remixing of content online. In Playful Commons, we experiment with play-positive guidelines and conditions for play in specific spaces.

Institutions love the idea until they realize it involves being okay with random people playing in "their" space, in ways they can't imagine and might not like to see. Sometimes, when partners are concerned that people might act like unruly or unsophisticated children, I recognize my own former skepticism.

So here's what I take away from these three short encounters with Bernie (experiencing him in action, in writing, and in conversation): Let's talk about the permissions we are willing to grant each other as adults. And let's base this conversation not on behaviors we would like to see or avoid but on compassion for the play of others.

Seen from this angle, permission ceases to be an administrative act where an immature person is allowed to do something risky under the watchful authority of "the adult in the room." Permission instead becomes the recognition of shared maturity—a maturity that includes experience in the never-ending, always-surprising practice of play.

A LIFETIME OF PLAY

FRANK LANTZ

Based on Bernie's participation in the New Games movement and its roots in '60s counterculture, you might expect his philosophy of games to line up neatly with the "hippie vs. square" political rhetoric of that era.[1] You might expect him to champion play, improvisation, and collaboration as rebellious and liberating forces fighting against the oppressive power of rules,

---

1   Adapted from remarks given on the occasion of presenting Bernie with the inaugural Lifetime of Play award at the Games for Change festival.

structure, and competition. But he's much too clever for that, much trickier. Bernie's thinking about games is far more subtle, nuanced, and complex.

Let me give you an example. In my Intro to Game Studies class we read a chapter from Bernie's amazing book *The Well-Played Game*. Here's a short quote from it:

> There is a very fine balance between play and game, between control and release, lightness and heaviness, concentration and spontaneity. The function of our play community is to maintain that balance, to negotiate between the game-as-it-is-being-played and the game-as-we-intend-it-to-be. It is for that reason that we maintain the community. On the one hand we have the playing mind—innovative, magical, boundless. On the other is the gaming mind—concentrated, determined, intelligent. And on the hand that holds them both together we have the notion of playing well.

There's a lot going on there. First of all, there's the joke (about having a third hand) and that's pure Bernie, to be making this deep and subtle point and to wrap it all up in a silly joke. But the point he is making here really *is* deep and subtle. In this passage he deftly sidesteps the temptation to fall into a simplistic dichotomy of good and bad—liberating play versus constricting rules. Instead he highlights the way these forces are always in a vibrant dialectical tension. A tension that is the result of the fact that both attitudes have good qualities, things we might want, but they can also come into conflict.

And the way he resolves this tension is by stepping back and reminding us that we play games for a purpose—to achieve a particular kind of pleasure, beauty, and meaning—and looking at this purpose helps us understand what's going on in a game, in the dance between games and players, rules and play. And the process of getting what we want out of this dance can be very challenging. It's not always easy and automatic; it can require our attention and effort and focus. And—most importantly— this process is never done alone; we always do it in collaboration with other people.

The most recent time I read Bernie's passage in class was while we were looking at famous game studies readings in the broader general context of twentieth-century intellectual thought. In particular we were examining the pervasive anxiety about how the modern, industrial world has transformed human life—the way our traditional structures of meaning have been upended and dismantled and replaced by systems of logic and science and technology, institutional frameworks that have an immense instrumental power but that can also seem cold, indifferent, or even hostile to the human values that matter most to us as individuals. This is, in some ways, the central theme of modernity.

And here in this passage we have a beautiful, hopeful way to think about this same dynamic—the dialectic of play and game is a lot like the dialectic of enlightenment. And if we want to think our way through this dilemma, which we desperately need to do, perhaps we can use the same approach by thinking about the larger purpose of our lives—about meaning and pleasure and beauty—a purpose that we can never discover on our own but only in dialogue with other people.

In my mind Bernie is a kind of moralist—not in the negative sense of someone scolding you for your mistakes, but in the positive sense of someone who encourages you to try harder and inspires you to keep trying, trying not just to be good but to figure out *what good is*. And this is why I think it's so important to read Bernie's work and teach his ideas. I, too, want to leave the world a better place than when I found it, and Bernie shows us how it's done.

GIRLS OWN THIS PLAYGROUND

KATIE SALEN TEKINBAŞ

At the start of my career writing about and designing games I ran across a little-known study on the social play of *Foursquare* (Hughes 1983). *Foursquare* is a playground game involving a red rubber ball and a grid of four squares. Players bounce the ball into the squares occupied by other players in the hope that they will be unable to bounce it back out. The study explored how a particular ruleset for *Foursquare* developed by a group of young children on a playground operated as shorthand for "playing nice."

Foursquare offered fertile ground for such a study because an individual player (the "king") calls a ruleset before each round of play. A call of "Rooie Rules," for example, meant that players were prohibited from doing such moves as "slams" (bounces high over a player's head) and "duckfeet" (being hit on the legs), along with a long list of other individual calls. Players were not expected to know the complete set of rules as the players all had a tacit understanding that Rooie Rules were "nice," and "nice" was of paramount concern. Anyone choosing to play had to accept and uphold a standard of social behavior disguised as the real rules of the game.

Bernie would have loved this research, as he wrote often and lovingly about the search for a well-played game: a game that holds a community together. School kids recrafting the rules of a game to reinforce the boundaries of an emergent, imagined, and ever-evolving social community is more than an act of the imagination; Bernie would claim it as an act of power.

In my intro to game design courses, I often pair this research with a reading from *A Well-Played Game*. Doing so helps me to frame Bernie's observation that "it is easier to change the game than the player" within both a technical and social framework. Changing the play of a game is a powerful way to reshape and reinterpret the world around us, but it doesn't always benefit everyone equally.

Power comes in many forms and in the case of Rooie Rules, it worked as a sorting mechanism, allowing some kids (mostly girls) inside while keeping other kids (mostly boys) out. Knowing what was "nice" was code for a complex set of gender and social relations that organized play between children on the playground. A call of "Rooie Rules" symbolized one's social status within a particular social circle. The expansion and complexification of the rules over time cemented friendships and signaled a growing center of power. Boys beware! Girls own this playground.

THE PRIVATE IMAGINATION

We are used to imagining alone. On a long train journey. Falling asleep. Sitting and drinking coffee. We even have conversations with other people in our head—playing both parts ourselves, summoning ourselves and other selves from our imagination.

In this section I'm going to talk about imagining on our own—why we do it, when we do it, different ways that we might perhaps sometimes want to do it. When our imagination works, and when it doesn't. How to strengthen our imagination, and why we might want to do that in the first place.

STRENGTHENING THE IMAGINATION

Maybe you're excited about the idea of strengthening your imagination—of just imagining, and getting better at it, and seeing what happens in your imagination and in the world.

Or maybe you feel a little bit strange about it, and you aren't sure how you would strengthen your imagination and what it would feel like. Maybe you can't quite imagine it yet.

But it's okay! As long as you're willing to give it a go, you can practice on your own, in your head, and nobody will have any idea. If you feel silly, that's okay. Nobody is watching you. If you feel too serious about it, then that's okay, too.

In fact, let's start not by imagining something, but by imagining that you're imagining. Let's start with a story of *Silly You and Serious You.*

SOMETHING TO PLAY: *SILLY YOU AND SERIOUS YOU*

This is a game you can play entirely in your head. You can also play it when you're outside and walking from one place to another, but for now I'm just going to ask you to play it completely and totally in your imagination.

Imagine there are two yous: Serious You and Silly You. Imagine what they might be like. Imagine the conversations they might have.

Silly You and Serious You are the two most opposite characters that ever had character. Serious You and Silly You are identical as identical twins, but inside they are very different. Silly You is just like you, but without any of the serious bits. Serious You is just like you, but without anything silly. Silly You and Serious You are as real and actual as you or I can be. Serious You and Silly You are as imaginary as you or I can imagine.

Now imagine perhaps that Serious You and Silly You are walking home, and when they're almost exactly two blocks from their front door, they both notice, at the same time, that there is really nothing else to do—nothing else, that is, except walking home. It isn't really that they're bored. Just that they've gone on that very same walk so many times before. It isn't really that there isn't anything to do. There are all kinds of things to look at: the sky and the clouds, the street lamps and the telephone poles, the houses and the people walking by, the cars, the birds. It's just that they need something new to do. And everything, even the things they hadn't ever noticed before, seems, well, old. All they need, really, is something else to be doing while they walk— something else to do or think about, just until they get home.

About half a block later, let's imagine that Silly You comes up with a silly idea. Wouldn't it be fun, Silly You says, to pretend that something, something really scary, is following us? Something really, really scary? Something that could catch us and eat us, in some kind of pretend way, completely up?

For the next half-block, Serious You thinks very hard (which, for Serious You, is just about the most fun you can have). Serious You thinks about the implications and ramifications, about being scared and about scary things and about the effectiveness of pretending to be afraid as an antidote to boredom. Serious You thinks about the pros and cons, the ups and downs, the ins and outs. In the meantime, Silly You thinks about the scariest possible things, and how fun it could be to pretend them into being—big things with lots of teeth and very, very bad breath.

And, at the very moment when they are each exactly one block from home, Serious You makes a decision. Yes, Serious You decides, pretending a scary thing into being would indeed be an effective distraction and simultaneously a meaningful exercise of the pretend muscles. And, by sheer coincidence, Silly You decides exactly at that moment what the Pretend Thing looks like, precisely what it sounds like, and absolutely how it smells.

That is, assuming you find smells scary. This is Silly You and Serious You, after all, not Silly Me and Serious Me. Maybe you, or You, or Yous will imagine something very different when you think about something scary. But bear with me for now, and imagine along with my imaginings about you.

So let's imagine that, for the whole next block, the closer Silly You and Serious You get to their house, the closer the Pretend Thing gets to them. When they're three-quarters of a block from home, they can almost see the Pretend Thing's teeth and eyes and claws. When they're half a block from home, the Pretend Thing is twice as close and the Pretend Thing's teeth and eyes and claws are twice as big. When they are a quarter-block from home, the Pretend Thing is four times closer, and the Pretend Thing's teeth and eyes and claws are four times bigger, and the Pretend Thing's breathing is four times louder and the Pretend Thing's breath is four times smellier. And, when they're an eighth of a block from their house, they can hear the Pretend Thing's toes scratching on the sidewalk. Eighteen toes. All on one horrible foot that smells even worse than its breath, which now smells eighteen times worse than it did before. It is now frightfully clear exactly how horrible its horrible smell smells!

And, by the time they're in front of the house, they can hear the Pretend Thing's terrible growl—like the growling of a big, angry, hungry, and very upset stomach. Just as they get to the door, Silly You is almost not pretending at all. Silly You is almost really, genuinely scared. And Serious You, even Serious You is getting just a little bit seriously scared.

And, just as they finally get the door opened, and the Pretend Thing has dug all of its eighteen pretend toes deep into the front step, and scrunched itself into one big, angry, smelling, gurgling coil of very mean muscle absolutely and totally ready to pounce and grab and bite—Serious You and Silly You jump into the house and slam the door completely shut right in the made-up face of the horribly pretend Pretend Thing.

"Wasn't that," says Silly You, shaking and sweating and breathing hard, "fun?"

SOMETHING TO PLAY: WALKING GAMES

Imagining something like the story we've just explored is the kind of imaginary journey you can take all by yourself, anywhere. Or if you'd like something with rules, something with a structure to help you start imagining, you could try (for example) one of the walking games found in Phil Smith's book *Mythogeography: A Guide to Walking Sideways*. These sorts of walking games can be a wonderful way to practice, to keep your imagination working.

Here's a bunch of walking fantasies Smith calls *Solo 'Splorin' Exercises*:

- You are Cupid. Match people in the streets.
- You are a diver. Explore the city as if it were underwater.
- You are a mist. Drift through the city.
- You are a fox in human skin.
- You are dead and gone to heaven/hell.
- The city is under occupation by intelligent microbes, Martian bodysnatchers, mind control rays—you can't tell the resisters from the wholly invaded. Do not attract attention to yourself. Choose routes where the least number of people will see you. Use alleys and back paths. Walk calmly through crowds. Show no emotions. Ignore commodities. Hide your hunger.

And here's one that he calls *Gum Galaxy*:

- Where the pavements are covered, like a rash, in chewing gum, use chalk to draw lines to connect the pieces of gum in stellar constellations. Name them in Latin (if you don't know any Latin make it up).

If we look around we can find walking games everywhere, in our heads and in the way other people behave as they walk. Haven't you played a walking game already? Followed someone thirty yards behind to help you decide where to go, or stepped over the cracks, or closed your eyes for a moment as you walked in the sun?

Try Yoko Ono's "City Piece" from 1963, which goes:

Step in all the puddles in a city.

Or her "Walking Piece," which goes:

Walk in the footsteps of the person in front.

1. on ground
2. in mud
3. in snow
4. on ice
5. in water

Try not to make sounds.

Or you can look at *Casual Games for Casual Hikers* by Harry Josephine Giles, which has games like *Stonypath*:

Establish a gentle walking rhythm. Without breaking it, kick a small stone ahead of you. Score the number of kicks you make before stumbling or losing the stone. Strive to score higher. When you leave a stone behind, remember to say goodbye.

Walk, perhaps, while inventing different ways that you could walk. Walk while looking. Walk while wondering. Wonder while walking.

FAILURE OF THE IMAGINATION

These sorts of walking games can help give us one answer to why we might want to imagine things. Imagination can help us to pass the time—it can make the world more exciting. We can turn a two-block walk where we are a little bit bored into a desperate chase where we barely manage to dodge the most terrible, disgusting, ravenous monster we can think of. And we can do that all on our own without needing anything from anyone else—without even letting anyone else know that we've done it.

But of course that's not the only thing imagination can do. And something that might make it easier for us to think about why imagination is important is for us to think about what happens when imagination fails.

First: what does it mean for our imagination to fail? And why does it matter? Of course none of us can imagine perfectly— even when we imagine how we, ourselves, might feel, we are often a little bit wrong. The things that happen in our imagination aren't the same as they would be if they happened outside our imagination in what we might want to call the "real world." But that doesn't mean our imaginations have *failed*.

In her post "The Curse of the Inability to Imagine," Tania Lombrozo writes:

> In imagining the future, we suffer from a curse of ignorance. Morse [one of the first developers of the telegraph] couldn't pos-

sibly have foreseen the precise course of technological innovation. But in imagining the past, we additionally face a curse of knowledge: We can't entirely remove the future possibilities that we know are yet to come. This failure can make the experience of living in the past seem more impoverished than it was, because our familiar technology isn't just absent, but missing. (I recently had to explain our rarely-used home phone to my young daughter: "It's kind of like Skype, only without the video.")

Her conclusion:

> But we know that people who grew up using rotary phones didn't experience them as defective cellphones. They were simply phones.
>
> And the first flip-phones were admired for their slenderness, not rejected for the additional diminution they had failed to achieve.
>
> This isn't to deny the possibility of visionaries—people with the creativity and daring to imagine how things could be different. Nor is it to ignore the real advantages and pleasures modern-day technologies can provide. But recognizing our limitations in imagining the past brings an important lesson in humility and in humanity: "They were just as we are, with less technology."
>
> And in most respects that matter, future people will be also—but with more.

So we know that we can't imagine perfectly. We get things wrong. But that's not a problem. That's to be expected. It's how imagination works, as Lombrozo points out—we can never entirely separate ourselves from the context that we're in when we imagine; we can never be quite "right."

And yet we can't deny the impact of "failures of the imagination." We use that term so liberally to explain so much about our world: why people are less empathic than they should be;

why we are destined to repeat history; why we succumb to greed, ambition, and intolerance; why we support slavery and other forms of human trafficking; why we can't accept people of different sexual orientations, different socio-economic status, who dress differently, act differently, think differently.

And often the failure here isn't that we imagined something and imagined it wrong. Often, the failure is that we *didn't even try*. If we really, truly try to imagine how someone else might feel, and try as hard as we can, then even if we get it wrong it might still be a success. It might still help us to understand or empathize or just accept a difference. It's only if we don't even try that we definitely fail.

You'd think, wouldn't you, that with all these failures we'd spend more time teaching people how to strengthen their imagination; we'd study people who seem to have exceptional imaginations and make them our teachers; we'd recognize, award, and support people (children, adults) for the brilliance and clarity of their imagination.

But we don't. Maybe because we're just too silly. Maybe because we just can't imagine how valuable a gift imagination can be.

SOMETHING TO PLAY: *BLATHER*

The next game I'd like to play is the first of a few different games on a theme of "blathering."

To blather is just to talk for a long time about something that isn't important, without stopping to think. When you are blathering, you are talking in "draft mode." There's no editing, no filtering, no reflecting. You just talk. You know you're doing it right when you surprise yourself with what you hear yourself saying.

In letting yourself do this, in letting your words drift along in the currents of thought, you can almost hear your consciousness streaming and meandering, freely associating whatever it feels associated with at the moment. At this level of listening, you are almost able to hear the voice(s) of your imagination. As if you're talking not so much in words, but in voices, in images. Like daydreaming.

And doing this aloud, alone or in the company of strangers—all of this becomes almost close enough to the surface for you to see it. Images swimming like minnows, sometimes becoming especially vivid, turning into gold as they meet the light of your awareness.

It's fun, doing this. It's play. It's a doorway to playing with Mind. And the longer you can think of it that way, as play, the freer your thoughts can be to form into visions, the deeper your words can sink into the dreamy depths of your limitless imagination.

Ever met people who just talk and talk and continue to talk even though no one is listening anymore? Not even themselves? You know, they just go on and on and then on some more?

It's kind of fun. For them, at least. As long as no one has to listen. It's a letting go. A stepping outside of the way people normally talk, outside of reason and logic and coherent speech. It's a way for people to hear themselves think. Which is also a way for people to hear their imagination at play.

It's something people can practice by themselves, especially when they're somewhere where they can be anonymous. Like in a crowd, or on a walk or run, or in the shower.

If you prefer, you can sing. To a melody you make up as you go along. To a pretend microphone. In a pretend shower.

So for this game, I'm going to ask you to do just that. Alone. By yourself. Talking and talking, or singing and singing, or singing and talking—without trying to make sense, without thinking about what you're going to say or sing. Spontaneous generation of the only slightly meaningful and/or totally nonsensical. Just for a minute, to start. And then maybe another minute, if you can.

FLOWING WITH IMAGINATION

This blathering game is maybe beginning to help us understand more about what might happen when imagination succeeds—what we can do with imagination and how and why.

When you're in the conceptual groove, you won't know what you're going to say until you've already said it. That's the goal of this little game. Because if you achieve that, you've managed to silence the inner editor, that critic, that judge. You'll be able to hear yourself think.

You might be familiar with the concept of "flow," as described by Mihaly Csikszentmihalyi in the 1970s. This is the state of mind where you're immersed in something completely, entirely involved, given over to the enjoyment of the activity itself. Csikszentmihalyi suggested that flow happens when our *ability* to do something is balanced well against the *challenge* of that thing—if the challenge is too high we get anxious, and if our ability is too strong we get bored, but if we are balanced in between then we are more likely to find ourselves *in flow*, a state of optimal experience. If we think about Bill Russell's game of basketball that we talked about earlier, there's the same feeling there: the perfect poise between two teams operating at their best, their ability and the challenge that they're facing becoming almost equal.

But there are many ways to get to that sense of being entirely absorbed by an activity, to conjure up our own immersion as we play or talk or think or run or write or whatever else we might get absorbed in. And one way is just—well, to blather. To find a trick to turn off the critical part of our brain and let our uninhibited selves out to play.

Because blathering is about using our imaginations and getting access to the parts of ourselves that we usually block off. The deep, strange truths. The discoveries. The things we find out about other people as well, once we begin thinking about them without the filter of our non-imagination getting in the way.

When something is silly, pretend, imaginative, or "just a game," then we can dodge around the bits of our brains that might stop us from realizing something, or noticing something, or feeling a connection.

And doesn't that sound good? Doesn't that sound worthwhile? Even better than turning the last two blocks of a walk home into an adventure—but it's all part of the same facility. If we get better at imagining, we don't just get better at passing the time and having fun on our own. We get better at understanding ourselves and other people's selves.

This happens almost by accident when we strengthen our imagination and when we try imagining things more often. But it's also an aspect of imagination that we can focus on deliberately. If we set our minds to it.

SOMETHING TO PLAY: *MAKING FACES*

To play this game, you need a mirror.

First, you get the mirror. Next, you decide on a face you're going to make: silly, stupid, wise, blissed-out, funny, lovely, angry, happy, ecstatic . . .

You close your eyes. Make the face. Then open your eyes.

Have a look at your face! Look at all the tiny details. How convincing is it? Is it the face you meant to make? Try making it again. The face that you're looking at. Make a face, close your eyes, then look at the face you made, and the next time try to make that same face, only even more convincingly.

I like playing this sort of game with myself. Maybe a more accurate descriptor for this activity might be "reflection." Yes. I like to reflect on myself.

I agree, it's an odd thing to be doing because when one reflects on oneself one often finds oneself wondering who, exactly, is reflecting on whom.

Here's another game you can play with a mirror—although this time, it doesn't need to be a real mirror. It can be an imaginary mirror if you like, though that might be harder to find than a real one.

First, we select two aspects of ourselves, like: mean and kind, happy and sad, serious and silly, pretty and pretty ugly.

Now, take out your imaginary two-sided mirror (for greater conceptual reference, it will henceforth be referred to as a "reflection device") (patent pending). If you can't imagine a two-sided reflection device, you can imagine a one-sided reflection device and a double-flip (see the following description). Or you can use a real one.

Look into your reflection device and make a face that is definitely one half of one of the pairs of yous: mean you, say. Take your time. And give it time. Until the face you see is inarguably, indubitably, and indeed the face of you, being mean (or happy, or serious, or ugly, or whatever you you'd like to try out).

Now flip your reflection device over, and do the same thing until the face you see there is most typically and unmistakably you, being the other side of yourself—in our example, you being the kindest you you've ever been. (Here's where, if you have a one-sided mirror, you must use the aforementioned double-flip, turning the mirror away and then back around.)

Now flip the reflection device back over and see if your first face is still as unmistakably mean (or whatever it was supposed to look like) as it was when you last saw it.

And flip the reflection device over again, and check out your other self. Check out your other other self!

And again flip and again flip, randomly, seeing if you can catch one of the versions of yourself off-guard.

THE IMAGINED AUDIENCE

One thing you may have found with your imagination is that you use it not just to imagine yourself but to imagine other people, even totally non-imaginary people that you know and see and spend time with.

Certainly I often find myself (wherever my self happens to be at the time) addressing an imaginary audience. I don't know if it's because I think a lot or write a lot, but, more often than not, when I'm supposedly alone with my thoughts, I'm imagining that I'm talking with or writing to this or that person or multitude.

One of the things I've realized about my imagination that I think you might also realize or want to realize or just think about is this:

Not only am I the dreamer of my dreams, but I'm also all the people I'm dreaming about. I'm the puppeteer, and each and every dream-being speaks with my voice.

It's a remarkably freeing thing to think about. And a lot more fun than what happens if you start believing that all those people inside you are someone else.

It's a fun, and maybe even enlightening, thing to think about: your imagined audiences. So, if it makes reading this any more fun, feel free to imagine me reading it with you. I've certainly been continuing to imagine you reading it.

There's an article by Eden Litt called "Knock, Knock. Who's There? The Imagined Audience" that shows just how powerful this imagined audience can be:

> The imagined audience is the mental conceptualization of the people with whom we are communicating, our audience. It is one of the most fundamental attributes of being human . . .
>
> The less an actual audience is visible or known, the more individuals become dependent on their imagination. Therefore, people are typically more reliant on the imagined audience during mediated communication, such as letter and email writing or talking on the phone, than in face-to-face settings.

Litt talks about research that shows that an imagined audience can be just as powerful as a real audience! When people are with us in our imagination, they can affect us even when they're not really nearby—even if they *couldn't* really be nearby because they're far away or busy or they've fallen out of touch. Even if they're fictional characters from books or movies we love, even if they're people we've made up in our own heads, even if they're real people we know who have died. Litt continues:

> For example, Fridlund (1991) found that participants smiled more, regardless of their happiness, when they were either watching a movie with a friend or when they believed a friend was watching the same video in another room than when they were alone or thought their friend was partaking in a different activity. He concluded, "solitary faces occur for the same reasons as public ones, if only because when we are alone we create social interactions in our imaginations."

And just think about how important this role of the imagined audience is nowadays, when so much of our social interaction is with an online audience. So much of the time we don't really know who our audience is—if we write a blog post, we can't know who is going to read it and respond, now or ten years from now. If we write a tweet, we don't know which followers are online, who has us muted, who might see whatever it is that we're saying and respond to it. So we have to make up our audience in our heads, even if we don't get it quite right. Of course, this can make things complicated! Let's hear from Litt one more time:

> Without being able to know the actual audience, social media users create and attend to an imagined audience for their everyday interactions. The imagined audience construct is worth understanding better because, while we are dependent on the imagination as a guide during social media use, it is the actual audience on the other side of the screen reacting and judging the performance. Therefore, potential tensions between the two audiences may lead

to consequential outcomes. The conundrum then becomes how do people's imagined audiences compare to their actual audiences? And what influences the alignment of an individual's perception of the audience with the actual audience?

Complicated, like I say! But isn't it wonderful as well? Our imagined audience isn't real but we can still get pleasure from them and feel things differently, just as if they were. We can relate to these imaginary people as if we were really with them and they were really real. No wonder imagination is so powerful! No wonder it's such a gift for happiness and understanding!

And because we can now understand that spending time with people in our imagination can be powerful and transformative, even when we know that all of the people are just ourselves, I'd like to finish talking about the private imagination with one more game.

This is a game for quite a few players, and maybe one day you'll play it in a group. But for now I'd like you to imagine someone else to play it with. You could imagine someone you really know, if you like, and how they might play. Or if you'd like, you can play with me, the version of me in your imagination, and I'll play with my imaginary version of you.

SOMETHING TO PLAY: *THE ORCHESTRA AND THE CONDUCTOR*

This game is a variation of another game from Augusto Boal's wonderful *Games for Actors and Non-Actors*. He writes:

> Each actor or group of several actors utters a rhythmic or melodic sound. The conductor listens to them. They must produce the same sound, whenever the conductor asks them with a gesture

of hand or baton. They must be quiet when she does not require their sound. In this manner, the conductor can compose her own piece of music. Everyone can have a turn at being the conductor.

Getting to be a conductor is at least as fun as getting to be an instrument, so it's important that Boal's recommendation ("everyone can have a turn at being the conductor") be graciously and continually offered.

This game, as Boal describes it, is most definitely fun as is. And it's a sort of fun where an imaginary audience is maybe even better than a real audience! With a real audience, you and the other players might have to worry about whether they're bored, how they're enjoying the sound, what the experience is like for them. If the audience is imaginary, though—well then! They can stand on their feet and roar, they can applaud, they can faint at the beauty of the music you're creating, they can stand on their seats and start to dance—why not?

It's also the sort of game that holds within it a whole myriad of other ways that you could try playing. Here are a few ideas:

Before the conductor starts, have everyone "tune up"—that way they, and the conductor, can get a sense of what sounds there are to play with.

Or: limit everyone to body or vocal sounds only, or body sounds and vocal sounds together, only.

Or: after players decide what instrument they want to be, have them organize themselves into sections (brass, woodwind, strings, percussion). You might also want to help the conductor create a gesture to indicate only one instrument or an entire section.

Or: appoint soloists (for a concerto, or double or triple concerto).

Or: decide on what era the music should come from. It could be from the future, of course.

Or: use words instead of sounds, each player using one word only. Then try it with two words or three for each instrument. Words from a poem. Any word the instrument chooses. Rhyming words only, nonsense words, sad words, happy words.

Or: make up your own way to play, and try it out.

Or: as you sit now, probably on your own, probably not playing this game yet, just think a little about what sound you might make if you were playing for real. And that imaginary person you're playing with? Think about the sound they might make too. And just make that sound out loud, under your breath if you prefer, and imagine that you're with that friend or stranger as you do.

SLOW PLAY

TRACY FULLERTON

When I met Bernie in 2004, I was already a fan of his work. Charged with a sense of academic seriousness, I invited him over to the University of Southern California to talk to our game design community about New Games and the history of this influential movement. Bernie took one look at us, with our prepared readings and notebooks, ready to capture the wisdom of his lecture, and said, "You're all too intellectual. Let's go outside and play."

And we did. We played *Prui, Rock Paper Scissors Tag, Hug Tag, Knots, Pattycake*, thumb wrestling, *Lemonade*, and *Dum Dum Da Da*. We played until we collapsed on the grass with laughter and joy. We opened ourselves up to Bernie's invitation to play and it changed our lives and our community of play and design forever. We still do it with every incoming class—we go outside and play together like Bernie taught us to do so long ago. I still have the tattered list of games he gave me that day, and every time we play, I try to channel Bernie's generosity of spirit as I introduce these new, and yet familiar, games to my students.

I am always overwhelmed each time we play these games together by the continual surprises that these deceptively simple games offer. The gifts they unwrap in each of us as players and designers. And since that day, I've carried within me the gift of Bernie's ideas, not as words on a page, or theoretical constructs, but as experiences that touch my imagination and inspire me in my work to always think first about the humanity of play, to lay aside the technological and the intellectual in favor of the emotional and the visceral.

One of the ways that I've always felt aligned with Bernie's philosophy of play is in his emphasis on the personal experience of a player. In his work, there is utmost respect for that private experience, even prioritizing it over the external aspects of play. So often, we point to the trappings of play—the cards and boards and software and controls—and we say, "There is the game." But for Bernie, and I feel this way as well, the game is not in those trappings at all—they are just the apparatus. The game, and all that it means to us, is the experience that we have while the apparatus is in use.

In his classic discussion of how we strive to play well, alone and together, Bernie defines the well-played game as one that is excellent because of the way it is being played. And the "wellness" that he describes is not focused at all on the trappings of a game or the outcome of its system, but rather on the holistic experiences of the players in the game, as it is played, before and after, and the personal meanings that are constructed throughout that process.

This focus on the personal, which is one of the most important ways that Bernie's ideas have affected my work, has led me to explore the design of digital games that are reflective in nature, using what I call "slow play." By this, I mean play that allows for, and even depends on, an internal and emotional process on the part of the player. This is play that nurtures that internal process through its design, its scope, and its pace. Examples of what I mean by slow play can be found in games I've made such as *The Night Journey* (2007) and *Walden, a game* (2017).

In *The Night Journey*, this slowness is coded into the experience: players can walk only at a slow pace at the outset of the game. Speed, and eventually flight, can only be gained through exploration and reflection on the game world. I felt that this initial restraint on the player would help them to engage with the details of the experience, the texture and grain of the visible world. Then, as they gained more freedom, and finally flight, they would understand the loss that accompanies such speed.

In *Walden, a game*, slowness is experienced as part of the natural arc of the in-game year that the game encompasses. The seasons pass and the world changes with each season. The player, out of necessity of living in this virtual nature, must fall into the rhythm of these changes and adapt to them. Each season holds its own challenges for survival and its own possibilities for sublime inspiration.

I'm interested in slow play not because slowness itself is equivalent to meaningfulness, but rather because the process of making meaning through reflection requires time at a human pace and cycles of response, interpretation, and unpacking of experience. I equate it in some ways to Bernie's call for an "interlude" in games, as he says in *The Well-Played Game*: "something that allows us to turn the game down—to turn the volume off just enough so that we can hear each other again." And, I would add, so that we can hear ourselves; so we can know ourselves in play.

EVER SINCE

ADRIAAN DE JONGH

Ever since I met Bernie De Koven, his view on play has defined how I interact with other people, how I wake up every day, go to work every day, cook my food every day. I pick my friends based on how much I can play with them. I practically freerun my way through the streets, playing with my environment. I see freedom in the rules around me, in the space that is left for me to play in.

Bernie's ideas on playfulness and social interaction have helped me understand that games create an opportunity for players to be playful, to be imaginative, to enjoy for the sake of enjoyment, to aimlessly fool around and wander, by themselves or with others. After I met Bernie, I started following his blog rigorously, reading all of his books, playing many of the games on his Funny Games list, and watching all of his videos, and I tried and still try hard to make Bernie's ideas central to my own game design practice.

Bernie has been a massive inspiration to every part of my career. If you look at physical interaction games I've designed like *Fingle* (2012) and *Bounden* (2014), you'll see that they underline Bernie's ideas on how physical interactions can lead to deep and profound social interactions and the ways that games can touch and transform the relationships between people. Many of my prototypes for future games are directly or indirectly inspired by folk game sessions I initiated or attended in which we played games from Bernie's Funny Games list.

And these are just the obvious examples of how Bernie has influenced my work. Even *Hidden Folks* (2017), a digital searching game I made in collaboration with illustrator Sylvain Tegroeg, has Bernie's ideas on player imagination at its core. The goal of the game is to find tiny people hiding behind or inside things by unfurling tent flaps, cutting through bushes, slamming doors, and poking crocodiles. Its miniature landscapes can have a thousand stories: some are made explicit so you know what to look for and can progress to the next landscape, but most are never made explicit and come to life entirely because of your imagination. The game doesn't reward you for finding those stories: the reward is purely in seeing them and inventing them as your eyes glance over the landscape.

ROLL WITH IT
GREG TREFRY

Play doesn't need much to take hold. Usually it just needs the right prompt to set the imagination loose. Maybe it's a simple image, like "the floor is lava!," that sends players jumping for high ground and their brains reeling with guesstimates of the distance between couches. Other times, a physical action triggers the imagination and points you toward play: bend your knees, bring your hands together, take a deep breath, and flick on your lightsaber. We want to bring our world to life through play. We just need an excuse and a tiny bit of imagination to help us get started.

Bernie knows this. Intuitively, I know this. I've been skiing for thirty years, and I still make race car noises as I hurtle down a mountain. But intellectually, I forget. I take the title of game designer too seriously. Rules and goals are my stock-in-trade. If I want the player to have fun, I have to tell them how to play, how to win, how to trade resources in the third round when the moon is in recess. Except I don't have to. I need to find the play and offer that up to their imaginations. I need to find the activity that is fun in and of itself. The activity that you do because it's too fun *not* to do. The action that gives you license to transform the world. Not rules or goals.

When I forget this, and go too deep into the system, I make myself stop and flip through a few of Bernie's games. They remind me that fun sprouts from a seed planted in the imagination. I read how to play a game like *Human Caterpillar* and remember that I don't have to read how to play this. To be honest, I'm not even sure I understand all of the directions. But I do understand the most important one, the seed: get down on the ground and roll around. I've "steamrolled" over my kids to screams of delight. I've rolled down hills, thrilling as the world turned from grass to sky to grass, faster and faster. I've also designed enough games to know that I'll probably never top that amazing kinesthetic experience through rules and mechanics alone. If I want to reach those dizzying heights, I need to work with play, not against it.

The simple descriptions of Bernie's best games always pull me back to this insight. Don't try to transform the world for players through brute force. Let them do it through their imaginations. The trick is to point people in the right direction. You don't always have to be a game designer. Sometimes you can accomplish more with less, if you're willing to put aside your ambition to be the designer and instead embrace the role of guide. Find an activity with potential. Set the stage. Bring your audience to the precipice of play. Plant the right prompt in their heads. And let them roll.

THE SHARED IMAGINATION

This section of the book is a very important section. It's about what we can do when we imagine together. When we do that, the possibilities are immense. Immeasurable. Really, truly, more than one of you, imagining together, means you're collaborating and cooperating and creating to imagine something that neither of you could have imagined alone.

We tend to think of imagination as something people experience in isolation, alone in some wind-swept place. So we have to make a concerted effort to help people experience how imagination functions as a shared faculty, even when they engage in it separately, but together.

But it's worth the effort. The image of the sole artist alone in his garret, though sometimes true, does not capture where the largest demand on creative effort usually takes place: creative teams busily and interdependently engaged in creative work. (Perhaps because it doesn't fit our image of an artist, there are few if any courses, programs, or services geared toward training creative teams to engage their collective imagination. And that's where our Imaginary University comes in.)

SOMETHING TO PLAY: *DARKROOM*

Let's start to think about shared imagination by playing a game.

It's a game for two or more players. But you're probably the only one playing right now. So please, like you did with some of the other games—just imagine you're not. As we've already learned, one way to make things more fun or more interesting is to play with the people in our imagination—even if those people are just ourselves in disguise.

This game is a bit like one of those story-building games you might have played, the sort of thing where people take turns to add a word or a sentence to what the last player said, only it's all about building an image instead. There's no story. No drama. Nothing changes or moves.

The game's called *Darkroom* because the image develops, like a photograph, in a tray full of developer. I like to play it while I'm lying down with my eyes closed because it's easier to imagine the image as it grows in detail.

It's a fun way to learn how to imagine something together, and that's basically the whole point of this book and especially games like this—having fun imagining together.

So, there we are. With our eyes closed. Imagining a photograph developing. Very slowly. So slowly that when the actual image begins to appear, we only get a hint of what the entire photograph might be.

You want only one person talking at a time and you want people to wait long enough between details so that everyone has time to let the picture resolve more fully in their mind's eye. The idea is to add the detail only when and as it appears to you. Sometimes people get inspired at the same time. You could make the rule that when two or more people feel called at the same time, the image is "developed" and that round is over. With a little mutual respect, and quite a bit of serendipity, this encourages everyone to keep an open door to participation while making sure that people "take their turn." On the other hand, it doesn't have to be a rule at all.

The first player starts with anything, say, "a fountain." Someone else (when so moved) adds a detail that he or she actually sees (in the mind's eye) when picturing a fountain.

Okay. This is crucial, central to the magic of the game: people only add details that they actually imagine. So, for example, you lie there with your eyes closed seeing the fountain, and you notice that you're seeing a marble fountain. Nobody said the fountain was marble. It could have been made out of rocks or crystal even. But you imagined a marble fountain, so you say something like "it's a marble fountain," and, hopefully, everyone's now picturing a marble fountain. Someone else, when picturing that marble fountain (it's a marble fountain now and forever more—until the game ends), notices that it seems to her that the marble fountain isn't working. No spray, no drips, even. Nothing. And it looks, in that player's mind's eye, very old. So she says: "It's not working and it looks very old." Again, the direction here is not to tell a story, not to try to be cute, but simply to say what you're seeing.

And you happen to notice, now that you see the old, broken, marble fountain, that there's green mold here and there, all over. But before you can say that, someone else notices that the whole thing has been painted white and says: "it looks like the fountain has recently been painted white." So that's what you see. And the mold goes away (perhaps it was painted over).

So far, nobody has actually said that the fountain being imagined is a water fountain. It could be any kind of white, old, broken marble fountain.

And then, for the fun of it, you find yourself saying something like "it's actually a white marble fountain pen."

Well, see, you might make people laugh, but you would also damage the spirit of the game. People can tell that you didn't actually see a white marble fountain pen. And even though you were indeed only joking, you took away (not purposefully, of course) the shared control and the essential honesty necessary for the game to be as fun as everyone wanted it to be.

So be honest. Be true to the images you're seeing. But as long as it's imaginary, and as long as you truly imagine it, the picture you build up together could be almost anything. It could be a photograph with sounds and smells. Maybe even taste—if you can imagine yourself licking it. Maybe you imagine that you can feel the bumps and nubbles and dust and stuff.

Therein lies the game of *Darkroom*.

It's not a storytelling game. It's not a joke-making game. Nothing moves. Nothing changes. Things just appear. Details. More and more details.

THE COLLECTIVE IMAGINATION

Did you play this time? In the real world, or in your imagination with someone else you were imagining?

I hope you did, and if you did, I hope you noticed something about what it means to imagine with somebody else. What happens when you imagine together.

Because *Darkroom* is not just about imagination. It's about something we might as well call "imagining together" or "the collective imagination" or the "public imagination" or, anyway, more or less "shared" imagination at play. At play!

I've been working with play and with games for a very long time now, as you heard earlier in the book. But it's only more recently that I've been thinking in depth about play as something that happens in our imaginations as well as in the world, something that happens in us and between us. And once I started thinking about that, I learned a lot of things.

I learned that our imagination is endless, without limits (unless we need it to have limits), without purpose (unless we wish it to have purpose). We can imagine anything to ourselves. Anything. And a lot of the time the things we're imagining are pictures, and those pictures aren't just in black and white. They can be in color. They can be in motion. They can be three-dimensional, holographic, surround-sound, wide-screen, aroma-rama spectacles accompanied by music of symphonic proportion. They can be, apparently, infinite. Not all of us see pictures inside our heads when we imagine. But we all have an infinite imagination. And the collective imagination, at play, when we don't just imagine to ourselves but to each other, for fun, is even infiniter.

I'm not talking here about art, or dance, or theater even. I'm not talking about someone picturing things for us. I don't even mean dreams, where we picture to ourselves. I mean where you and I and everyone we can imagine are imagining whole worlds together, for the fun of it.

Not for religious purposes. Not for social or governmental or scientific purposes. But for fun. Together.

That's where games come in.

And so do I.

And so, I imagine, do you.

Children seem to love imagining things together. They play school, house, doctor, train, creating shared fantasies, making them up as they go along. For all their love, though, they lack many of the social skills they need to have the fun they hope to experience. Often, one child takes over, taking too much responsibility and control for the unwinding of the fantasy to everyone's detriment. Arguing and sometimes fighting seems to become an almost essential part of the fun. But all too often it degrades into something far less fun than they intended.

Adults have all the skills for imagining things together that they did as children, plus they have the sophistication needed to keep everyone included, giving everyone an equal share in the creative control necessary to build a rich and rewarding fantasy—far richer than they were able to create as children. Unfortunately, though they have the skills, they all too rarely have the opportunity to exercise them. So things tend to fall apart.

If you really play *Darkroom* with someone else, it's an exercise as well as a game. It helps to establish a precedent for how to share in the creation of imaginary worlds. It helps to train us in imagining together, accepting and building on the imaginings of others. And that brings us to our next little section . . .

COLIBERATION

Imagination isn't something that just takes place in our dreams or fantasies or creative endeavors. It is much more central to our lives as human beings than that. It is the faculty that makes society possible.

So as we consider this section of the imaginary syllabus, I'd like to explore an experience that, for me, has been central to most of the understanding I've achieved in my lifetime explorations of the nature of things like fun and games, play and playfulness, self and society. It's an experience that you'll have touched on just a little if you played *Darkroom*, or any of the other games in this book, or even just imagined playing them. But it's also an experience that you will be able to recognize, if you're lucky, from your own time in the world.

What is this magical experience? I like to call it "coliberation." You may recall that I mentioned coliberation once before, when talking about that magical game of ping-pong I played with Bill Russell. I think of it as a shared transcendence of personal limitations, of our understanding of our own capabilities; a sudden, momentary transformation of our awareness of the connections between ourselves, each other, and the world we find each other in, between the actual and the imagined.

Let's look at the concept in more detail.

A shared transcendence: Something we experience in certain moments of playing with children and animals, standing in a storm together, floating in the ocean together, listening to and making music together, making love, watching a movie together, walking in the woods or on a mountain, eating a meal, reading a book, playing a game together, laughing together, dancing together, where the actual and imagined are one.

. . . *of personal limitations, of our understanding of our own capabilities*: An unsustainable union where distinctions between self and community, mind and body, actual and imagined—between whatever separates us from each other—are set aside to reveal the environment in which we discover each other.

. . . a sudden, momentary transformation of our awareness of the connections between ourselves, each other, and the world we find each other in: Sudden, momentary, and unsustainable because we must ultimately return to ourselves, to "minding the store." Sudden, momentary, unsustainable, spontaneous, undefining, transforming.

We return changed, not the same person we were: our understanding of who and what we can become, our very selves, our relationships—redefined.

"Coliberation" is a made-up word, and I am the maker-upper. It's a word I coined so I could describe to people what a "good meeting" is like: coliberation.

Coliberation is not the opposite of codependence. Coliberation is why we become that way. Why we seek each other out in the first place. What we have to give each other when we are at our best.

Coliberation is what happens when we work or play extraordinarily well together. Like on a basketball team or in an orchestra, when we actually experience ourselves sharing in something bigger than any one who is present. This is what I call the experience of the "Big WE." It's a corollary to the "Big ME" experience of self-transcendence. If the Big ME is a "peak experience," coliberation or the Big WE is like becoming a whole mountain range.

Even the relatively little WE is something found in a different dimension than the ME. It's the oddly tangible, yet essentially imaginary experience of relationship, of connection, of community. Oddly tangible because it can't actually be found in any one of us but only in the actual, though imagined, experience of both or all. It's a collective consciousness of which we may be only dimly aware and yet completely embraced by, identified by and with. And when this WE is so engaged as to form a solidarity, a oneness, and when the will of the one is one with the will of the many, it becomes transformed, and we with it.

I know I've experienced it in games and sports and the performing arts and at play. And, what makes me especially hopeful is that I've also experienced it in business meetings.

Coliberation's shared transcendence can make you feel just about as big, ME-wise and WE-wise, as you can get. Larger than life. Enlarged by each other's largesse. Beyond time.

Allow me to illustrate with this graph-like chart.

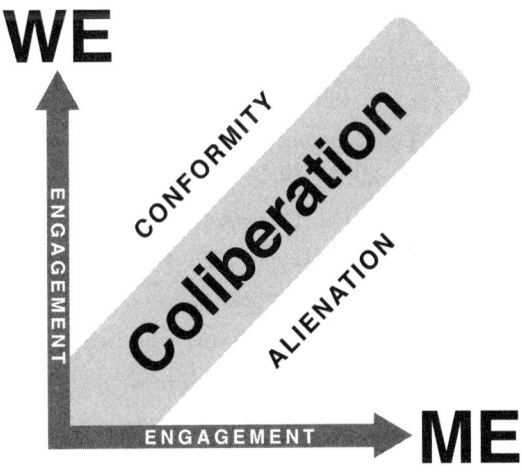

It's a little like Csikszentmihalyi's famous "flow" chart, but with "ME" and "WE" as the elements that lie in relation to each other rather than "Skills" and "Challenge." Perhaps another way to think about coliberation is to think about it as the social experience of being in flow together.

We talked a little about Csikszentmihalyi's conception of "flow" in the last chapter. It's the idea that in order to have an optimal experience, to be "in the zone," we need to balance our feeling of *being challenged* against our *ability to meet that challenge*. When something is at just the right difficulty level that we can manage it—but not so easily that we can let our attention wander or get bored—then we are *in flow*. And as our ability gets greater and the challenge gets deeper, so is the experience of being in flow ever more satisfying.

Similarly, for this chart, the higher or farther out we go on each axis, the more fun, the more complete it feels to be a ME or WE. The closer in, the less.

When the WE and ME are in balance, there is mutual empowerment—coliberation. This is indicated by a channel, diagonally equidistant between ME and WE. Here the good meetings, the well-played games, the fun things happen.

Fun is the background, the context, the steady state. Games are the activities that help us move up or down the channel, toward and away from the Bigger ME or the Greater WE.

When coliberation is at its best, so are we.

The term "coliberating" is a play on words, of course. Because it almost sounds like something beyond "collaborating." Yes, indeed, those moments in which we have actually managed to free each other from whatever constraints we usually impose on each other, these are truly and actually what you would call coliberating.

The experience of coliberation becomes more powerful as each participant becomes more thoroughly engaged, more wholly involved, and as the group itself becomes more unified, more engaged. Given the wholeness of the self and the group, we approach something beyond coliberation, beyond the game or meeting itself. Some coincidence of selves that undefines the limits of our capabilities. A coincidence having almost nothing to do with the game or meeting, and everything to do with the human spirit—shared moments of unusual clarity, vivid communication, and spontaneous combustions of understanding.

It's almost silly to have a word like this because all liberation is coliberation. You just can't liberate yourself by yourself. You can't be free if you're the only one. You can meditate, but you can't separate. You can become one only if you become "one with."

But as long as there is such a word as "codependence" and it makes something clear, well, then, we need a word like "coliberation" to make something else clear. Just as we now understand how we can sicken a relationship by becoming too dependent on each other, we can rediscover how we can heal a relationship by setting each other free, and we can understand how mutually healing things like play and teamwork and human relationships can become.

SOMETHING TO PLAY: *GROUP BLATHER*

To start thinking about this, let's return to *Blather*, the game we talked about earlier. But this time, instead of blathering alone, let's think about doing it in a group. Talking—just talking—without filtering anything or thinking about what you're going to say. Talking and finding out what words come out.

As you probably already figured out from the title, this game is just like *Blather*, only you do it in a group.

So you try blathering together, as if you were talking, but not actually talking to each other. Talking and listening at the same time, without trying to make sense of either. You can do it with five or ten or fifty people, everyone just milling around aimlessly. The goal is the same as when you play on your own. But if you can get the feeling right, it's a little easier. A little more fun. Because your inner dramatist is, for the moment, drowning in the sweet cacophony of unrehearsed thought.

After a while, certain strange and mystical things begin to appear. And then disappear.

One way to play this is to find another person in the group and to start talking. And keep talking. And while you're doing that, see if you can ask each other questions. And answer questions. And all the while, doing that basic non-stop blather thing.

Perhaps you might find yourself saying something like:

Hi there, gosh, it's really good to meet you I don't think I got your name Mine is Bernie I think it's about 3:13 according to my new Apple Watch Say haven't I seen you before O wait I think we were playing something together about fifteen minutes ago Gosh I'm so embarrassed Trish Delish You must have some pretty silly friends.

Excuse me Do you know what time it is I was just wondering because this game is getting a little silly and so am I My name is Tricia but my friends call me Trish Delish Really 3:13 already Wow, that's a great watch I've heard about those Apple Watches It's nice to meet you too Bernie No I don't think we were playing before

You're not trying to have a conversation in the normal way of things, but you do listen and respond and let the other person's imagination and blather run into yours. The more you ask each other, or comment on what the other person has said, or just compliment each other, the more fun, and the deeper and stranger, the game gets.

Another twist on the rules might be to get a bunch of people together—enough to feel like you're at a cocktail party. And, yes, if you want to add verisimilitude to the whole experience, you can get cocktails for everyone. Unlike a cocktail party, though, you: 1) are blathering, so you never stop talking, and 2) you're pretty much mingling all the time. You could make it the rule that if you're really enjoying blathering with a particular person, you can continue circulating together.

And if it happens, as it often does in cocktail parties, that you are blathering with something like a bunch of people at the same time, well, then, it's even more fun is what it is.

OF ME AND WE

The experience of relationship, the phenomenon of "WE," is at least as complex and as mystery filled as that of the experience of "ME." When we experience "WE," we experience something that includes, but is not, ourselves. It is not an experience of "otherness" because we are part of it. But it is not the experience of self because it is imagined. It is, nevertheless, an experience. As actual as the experience of "ME." If anything, it is the experience of a transcendent ME that is so ME-transcendent that it's part of a collection of other selves, also transcending.

ME-awareness is ultimately subjective, the very definition of subjectivity. Though I know that you probably have as strong an experience of what you call ME as I have of what I call ME, my experience is utterly opaque to you, as yours is to me. ME is identity, the voice with which you speak, the organ with which you interact with the world.

WE is something else. It's what you might call a shared subjectivity, this WE experience. Shared imagination. So strange, such a fundamentally fascinating mystery that that may in fact be what draws us to celebrate it so profoundly, in sports, religion, love.

And our relationship to that experience is even stranger. If I'm being all transcendent, so inextricably identified with all those other transcending selves, well, then, who is this "ME" that's doing all that experiencing?

Well, "ME" is a relative term. Even alone, shipwrecked on a deserted island with nothing more than a volleyball to keep you company, when there is no other, you create one so that you can be yourself again.

Sometimes when I talk about this I like to use an animated depiction of WE turning into ME turning into WE to capture that sense of relativity. In some very real sense, ME is always understood only in relationship to WE—the actuality of the self understood only in relation to the imagined other. And, likewise, the idea of WE loses all meaning if we try to take ourselves out of context.

Coliberation is what happens when you are fully engaged, yourself, in a community, actual and imagined, that is fully engaged. When you are so much part of the team that you are more fully yourself than you can be alone. When you are playing better because of the people you are playing with, and the people you are playing with are playing better because of you.

Coliberation is ME and WE.

Just listen to what Dr. Daniel J. Siegel writes in his blog post "The Self Is Not Defined by the Boundaries of Our Skin":

> I believe (and cannot find any science to disprove) that an important aspect of the mind can be defined as an embodied and relational, emergent self-organizing process that regulates the flow of energy and information both within us and between and among us.
>
> In short, the mind is an embodied and relational process that regulates the flow of energy and information.
>
> If this proposed definition of the mind is true, then the mind is certainly not simply "enskulled" and coming only from the activity of the brain, but it is at least embodied, and likely relational as well. And then the self, as an aspect of the mind, is not only embodied, it is also relational. This is the scientifically grounded view of why I say simply, "the self is not defined by the boundaries of our skin."
>
> The implications of this idea are fascinating. Of the many, one that stands out for me is the interpersonal emotional experience of empathic joy, the way we can feel joyful with others' joy, success, and happiness. Can you imagine a world in which we cultivated empathic joy instead of aggressive competition? Imagine if we could harness, for example, the courage and creativity of adolescents to take their essence of an emotional spark, social engagement, novelty, and creative explorations and have them compete with the world's problems in a collaborative way with each other. When someone succeeds and the enemy is beaten, everyone wins.

When we help others, we all win. Compassion and empathic joy are the outcomes of integration. And these are the realization of the fact that our "self" is both embodied and relational—we are more than the boundaries of our skin.

And with this integrated way of being, we all can reap the benefits of living authentically and cultivating connection with a deeper and wider sense of self as a MWE. MWE can do this, and together we will!

SOMETHING TO PLAY: *SIGNIFYING NOTHING*

The connection between ME and WE, between self and community, is pretty much what this book is about and for.

There's a game that I often use to start out a game session in order to illustrate this very truth. There are at least two different names for this game: *Signifying Nothing* and *The Sound and the Fury*. You, of course, are invited to make your own (maybe even better) name for it. I'm going to talk about this game, how to make it work in a group, how to make it fun for others, and how to use it to give a greater chance of cultivating this experience of MWE.

Everybody stands in a circle, facing in. One player, probably you, starts the game.

First, you exemplify as follows:

Make a sound (use your voice or tongue or lips or slap any handy body part—preferably, though not necessarily, your own). At the same time, move yourself in whatever way feels sufficiently random or appropriate. You could, for example:

- Snarl like a lion while crouching and showing your fangs and claws
- Pirouette like a ballet person while humming the first the first few measures of "Swan Lake"

- In a cat-like manner, lick your paw and rub saliva on your face while meowing

Then you explain that everyone should attempt to do more or less exactly what you just did, all at the same time. As close to immediately thereafter as possible, the person to your right (or whatever direction you've established) performs their own noise-accompanied movement (or movement-accompanied noise depending on personal priorities); everybody else again responds simultaneously with a close approximation of what the initiator did; after which, more or less immediately, the next person to the right of the person that was the last initiator does their thing, and so on; and also so forth, each person in the circle getting to be initiator, until it's your turn to start the next round.

If, on their turn to initiate a new sound-accompanied movement, a player cannot think of something to do, or just simply doesn't feel like it, they should, of course, pass. It's not a game if anyone feels they have to play. So, if by the time it's your turn again and nobody has passed, you introduce the possibility and demonstrate the passing sound and motion. Here are a couple suggestions:

- Bow, or curtsey, and say "ta-da" like a circus performer
- Cross your arms over your chest and clear your throat

Or, better yet, ask the group to come up with a better idea—another sound/motion combination, but this one reserved for the act of not playing.

From then on until the very last player has had a chance to initiate and send a new sound/movement around the circle, you try to respond as quickly as possible in a manner sufficiently ostentatious as to encourage other players to follow suit. Increasing the speed tends to add a certain sense of pressure that can, in turn, incentivize participants to do something really random and silly. The more spontaneous, the merrier.

If someone seems flustered, remind them of the passing gesture.

The whole idea is to make people feel that there's nothing they can do that's "wrong." You may need to remind them of it by modeling wrongness (which is also fun). What happens if you act out of turn, or perform the wrong gesture?

As the game progresses, you might also, when it's your turn, take several steps toward the center of the circle, or walk to the center, pirouette, and then walk to the opposite side of the circle—just to make things even funnier.

One by one, everyone gets to be the leader. Seeing the sound/movement that you invented repeated by the entire circle is always a bit surprising, and comforting. It's like you've not only been listened to but accepted, appreciated, embraced by the whole group, even. It's funny, and you've been perpetrator of that funniness. Your performance of the leader's actions affirms your place within the group, and the group's response to your leadership makes you feel not only safer, but more willing to do something spontaneous, silly, creative.

It's an experiential metaphor for the play between the individual and group, the movement between the isolation of leadership and inclusion in community. And as it continues, the fun becomes more and more extraordinary—spontaneous, shared, empowering, accepting, freeing—at nobody's cost, for everyone's gain.

Group Blather and *Signifying Nothing* are both very simple games, but when we just talk and listen together, or watch and respond and see ourselves accepted, we start finding out all sorts of things—about ourselves, about each other, and about how we can imagine together. All based on a little bit of play.

You don't need to play games in order to experience the power of coliberation. But it can help. It can be a shortcut.

And it's a place worth getting to, whether you take that shortcut or not. Coliberation is the win-win that is potential in every relationship, between friends, partners, strangers, generations, genders, even different species. Playing fetch with your dog, pushing a toddler on a swing, dancing with whoever happens to be close enough to you on the dance floor, playing in an orchestra, working with a surgeon in the operating room, meeting a stranger in a chat room, tweeting and retweeting, commenting and being commented on. All of these, when they are at their best, are coliberating. You make it easier for me to say what I want to say, to dance the way I dance best, to join, to quit, to join again.

Before we get too enthused about the ubiquity of opportunities to share an experience of coliberation, it is useful, if depressing, to note that the opposites of coliberation are even more ubiquitous. Coliberation is far from the norm. It is an optimal condition. But not, oh so not, the norm.

You walk in the park, and the one person who makes eye contact with you doesn't return your smile; you wait tables and one customer doesn't leave a tip or acknowledge the depth and elegance of your service; the person who bumps into you doesn't apologize; we don't notice an acquaintance waving at us so we don't wave back. It's so easy for the smallest thing to interrupt us on our way to coliberation.

I've noticed two of what you might call "boundary risks" for the experience of coliberation—two ways that the attempt to reach coliberation can go wrong. You may recall these risks from that chart we looked at earlier showing how coliberation is a balance between ME and WE. On one side, when the experience of ME looms too large, you get alienation. Sure, sure, you're all playing in the same orchestra, marching in the same band, but you don't really feel a part of it. It's like nobody is really listening to you, nobody is even aware of you. So the very experience that offers the opportunity for self-transcendence becomes one of isolation, alienation, of making you feel small, actually smaller than you are. There you are, all full of enthusiasm and good will, radiating energy and love and willingness to engage, and there they are, over there, way, way over there. And even though your self was just about as actualized as it could possibly get, the actuality of how you are being treated (or not) is crushing.

The other boundary risk, if WE becomes too powerful, is what you might call conformity. You are so much a part of the group, so thoroughly embraced, so totally identified with the group that you find yourself doing things that you, personally, would never do—except somehow you are. You get lost in the group, your own will, your own sense of self abandoned to the will of the many.

So when we try to encourage coliberation, we need to be aware of these two risks on either side—the ways that coliberation can go very wrong. More deeply wrong than when we just fail to reach that state in the first place.

When we suggest an exercise or a game or we get people working together, we need to think about what the risks are as we search for the wonderful middle ground where we can invent and be together.

This is another way that games can help us—they are structures for being together and making things together that have been refined and experimented with and that allow us to play or not to play as we like.

SOMETHING TO PLAY: *MOVING PICTURES FOR THE COMMUNITY THEATER*

Take, for example, *Moving Pictures for the Community Theater*. This is what we might call phase two of the game *Darkroom* introduced in the beginning of this chapter.

It's a game of the imagination in which you and your friends invent together, allowing whatever it is you each see to become part of whatever it is that you all see, until you all see the same, richly detailed image.

But this time, it's a moving picture.

I like to play this where people can be relaxed, sitting or lying down, eyes closed, close enough to hear each other easily. Sometimes we sit in a circle with our backs to each other. Sometimes we lie on our backs with our heads almost touching. Sometimes we lie on each other's tummies. We are all creatures of our bodies, and finding ways for our bodies to be near each other and comfortable is one of the best ways to make coliberation more possible. So there we are, together, comfortable. Sharing a quiet time. Allowing an image to appear, like Venus out of a shell, an image born of our collective imagination.

To start with, so that the moving pictures don't get too complicated, I like to use the idea of an animated gif, one of those cute looping videos you get in emails or on social media—but in our version of an animated gif, you don't just have the moving picture. You've got sound if you want it, and smell, and any other sense that you might like to add.

The shortness of the looping video is important. Part of the effectiveness of the *Darkroom* game is that it restricts everyone to imagining a photograph. The idea is not to tell a story, but to capture a moment. With a photo, we're talking about an instant. With an animated gif, we're still talking about just a few seconds.

The inclusion of motion and the invitation to the other senses results in an image that is much more moving, so to speak. More evocative. Capable of portraying an action and interaction. Still not a story (that would make it a very different game). But a moving picture. A moment captured. But a moment that lasts a few seconds.

Involving the other senses invites a more total presence, the creation of an image that can portray the experience of being in a hurricane, for example, or in a meeting.

If you like, you can start by coming up with a title for the moving picture. Framing the image as, for example, "the best conference ever" or "the unforgettable date" adds a qualitative dimension to the group creation. The picture you come up with can take on elements of reality, of possibility, that are far more moving than a mission statement or a floor plan, if you know what I mean.

But the play remains the same as in *Darkroom*. You sit (or lie, or lean), and when you feel you see something crystalize in this collaborative imagining, you speak out and add it. You are not consciously inventing. You are describing. You are noticing. You are building on what other people have said and incorporating it into your vision. You are coliberating.

ENCOURAGING COLIBERATION

So, imagining together is a wonderful thing. I hope I've convinced you of that. But it's not always an easy thing. And one of the aims of this chapter of the book is not just to convince you of this wonderful thing, but to talk about how you can make this wonderful thing happen. To suggest some games and exercises and ways of being that you can use to encourage people to imagine with you, or to get a group of people imagining together.

When I taught sixth grade at the Media Friends School in Media, Pennsylvania, I had the opportunity to experience a wonderfully sublime format for sharing a kind of collective spirituality in the Quaker Meeting. Here's a brief description, originally written by Hans Weening, available on the Quaker website:

> Silence is greatly valued by Friends. In removing pressure and hurry, it helps them to be aware of the inner and deeper meaning of their individual and corporate lives. It enables them to begin to accept themselves as they are and to find some release from fear, anxiety, emotional confusion and selfishness. This silence is more than an absence of sound: one can be aware of external sounds, such as a dog barking, a car passing, or a child calling. But these sounds are not distractions. They are absorbed, often unconsciously, as Friends try to be open to that of God within. An early Friend, Robert Barclay, described his experience during a meeting for worship as follows: "I found the evil in me weakening and the good raised up."

The seating for a meeting for worship is usually arranged in a circle or a square to help people to be aware of one another, to be conscious of the fact that they are worshipping together. Those present settle quietly, and by corporately seeking God's will, become open to one another. This may happen quickly, or it may take most of the meeting, usually an hour long.

Just like with games, we can see how tiny details such as how seats are arranged, the words that someone uses, and the time that people have to think can make such a big difference to how safe and involved they feel, how free they are to let their minds roam.

The silence is different from that experienced in traditional, solitary meditation, which normally takes place deep inside oneself, as a devotional exercise for one's own spiritual development. The listening and waiting in a meeting for worship is a shared experience in which worshippers seek to meet God.

Friends may worship entirely without words, but usually there will be some brief spoken contributions. This "ministry" is intended to express aloud what is already present in the silence. Anyone may feel the call to speak, man, woman or child, Friend or first time visitor. There is a very wide variety of sources of spoken ministry and the acceptance of them is an important part of Quaker worship.

The structure of the Quaker Meeting proves to be one of the most effective ways I've found to introduce people to the experience of the shared imagination. And the idea that anyone *can* talk—but that nobody *must* talk—is one of the things that can make games of the imagination so powerful. Nobody is forcing anything. Instead, you are letting things happen.

Of course, there's no spiritual purpose to *Darkroom*, unless you think having fun together counts as spiritual (and I'd certainly agree there). But isn't it wonderful to find that the same methods can be used in such different contexts to encourage all these different ways of being together?

There are other tiny details that can help encourage coliberation to emerge. When I play *Darkroom* and its variants, I like to ask people to get close—as close as possible—in a somewhat intimate position that will allow them to speak without necessarily seeing each other. Maybe with their hands in the air, or even their feet. Sometimes it's more fun if they aren't using their hands—just lying down, on their backs or tummies, heads together.

I don't mean to get too serious about this—just serious enough. After all, these exercises I'm suggesting are games. For, you know, fun. Something to play. And though you need to take it seriously enough to make it and keep it a "real game," it's still just a game.

And yet when you play *Darkroom*, like all of those games that play with the collective imagination, there's something mysterious about it, something profound, spiritual, you might say. There's something different.

If you can get people sitting and being together and understanding the powerful idea that talking or standing or actively playing is allowed but not mandated, then you can get them to begin to play together.

SOMETHING TO PLAY: *ZEN COUNTING*

Zen Counting is a marvelous game to get people comfortable and to help them understand that play is possible but not required.

I learned it from the local contingent of an organization called Peace First. The idea, which is very simple, is for a group of people to try to count from one to ten together.

If you're running this game, if you're using it to get a group to start playing together, then ask everyone to sit or lie down close to each other and close their eyes. And then, when someone is so moved, she can begin the count: one.

Someone else then continues to the next number, whenever he is moved: two.

The trick is to get to ten without two or more people saying a number at the same time. If they do, you have to start over from one.

It's not easy. And importantly, it's no one person's fault when it doesn't work. It's more an opportunity for people to play with the silence between the numbers. To grow more sensitive to it so they can anticipate when just the right amount of time has elapsed for the next number to be spoken and then to say that number first.

It can get frustrating. But it takes two to be wrong, so it's never something you need to take personally.

It's not about imagination as such, but about responding and thinking and listening, and it's a wonderful game to help people start to feel comfortable with being together and playing together and the places that might lead.

SOMETHING TO PLAY: *HANDLAND*

Handland is another simple game, but a slightly more challenging one. It invites people to make up what the game is about and how to play it. It emerged during an evening session at a weeklong seminar I was leading at the Esalen Institute, but it was more *discovered* than it was *invented*.

The only instructions are:

1. Get in groups of, oh, say three to maybe, I dunno, eight? ten?
2. Lie on your backs, in a circle, and slither toward the center until your heads are almost touching. More than almost touching is okay, too.
3. Raise your arms.

Really. That's the whole thing. But as you'll see if you try it, those rules are enough to invite people to create and share a world inhabited by disembodied but clearly friendly hands whose only purpose is to play together.

If things seem a little slow to start, you can just, you know, shake hands with your fellow handland occupants. You could pretend you're all hosts at a party and introduce some hands to other hands that seem to be close at hand. You could see if you could lure your fellow hands into a dialogue with something handy: pinkies, perhaps. Engage in a hand ballet, a square dance, a waltz. Or think of your hands as birds or fish or wormy things. Or see if you can create a hand basket and think of what you might put into it and to whence you might carry it.

At any rate and in sum, the idea here is to explore, invent, investigate the sense of the strange and all the other ingredients of playfulness that are therein implied; get out of the way, and let the hands find their own purpose.

TILT-MATE

IAN BOGOST

My college roommate had been a ranked, competitive chess player in high school. He wasn't very good at chess by global standards, but he was much better than me. He won every time we played.

Eventually, sick of losing, I asked him if there was anything I could do to win. I never assumed that I could become an effective chess player by some shortcut—I understood that real expertise required commitment and practice. My friend had an answer: He knew of an esoteric way to win a chess match without achieving a checkmate. All I had to do was upend the chessboard in a fit of impatient anger. As the pieces hurl asunder, the player who causes the chaos announces the victory by name: tilt-mate!

Admittedly, tilt-mate is not a canonical winning condition for chess. But for those who adopt it, it offers a new view onto it. Chess is a game known for a mathematical depth that demands deep planning or second sight. To play chess poorly is to fail to think effectively enough to play it well. As the stereotype goes, it demands mental prowess that contrasts with the brawn useful in sports or other physical contests.

Tilt-mate inverts that idea. It makes brawn central to chess, but as a counterpoint to its formal braininess. Thanks to tilt-mate, it becomes possible for impatience, caprice, and physical exertion to win chess, too. Admittedly, that victory comes at a cost. A winner by tilt-mate can make no claims to the mental proficiency that the "traditional" chess master puts on show. Some would say that it's a shameful victory—indeed, many would wonder how tilt-mate could be a victory at all.

I wondered as much for years, even after having tilt-mated my way to success many times. I finally found an answer in Bernie De Koven's *The Well-Played Game*, which of course had been there waiting for me for decades by the time I stumbled on it.

Writing about the virtues of clarity and practice in games, De Koven insists on the assent of the community of players before a game can be played well. This requires forging equity among a game's players. The "practice game" offers one approach: a game played before the game is fully comprehended by all its players. In this mode, "our objective is not to win, or even to play well," De Koven says, "but to make certain that everybody understands the rules." Only when everyone understands them can the game begin in earnest.

At first, the "practice game" struck me as a pedagogical tool alone. A way to get someone new up to speed, as hastily as possible, before moving on to the good stuff. To the real game. But reflecting on tilt-mate made me see the practice game anew. De Koven's idea is actually much bigger and more flexible than I had thought. Understanding the rules doesn't just mean inculcating them into a new or incompetent player. (After all, had my roommate repeated the rules of movement in chess, or offered reference to standard openings or techniques, I would have become no better at the game than I was already.) It can also mean altering the game completely, amending the rules such that a less competent player (that's me) develops a sensation of pleasure and mastery akin to that of another, more adept player. Playing well needn't mean playing the game "properly" but instead always means playing the game with a common understanding among its participants.

Tilt-mate transformed chess into a practice game for me. And decades after I learned it, I haven't stopped practicing. I'm still pretty bad at chess, and I don't think I'll ever get better. That's fine. Even if I rarely hurtle the board and pieces to the floor anymore, knowing that it's an option makes the game appealing. Without that appeal, I'd never be able to play in the first place. The "real" game need never start. Who cares? It's more important to play the game well than to play it right.

FOCUS ON THE FUN
ZACK WOOD

Over the past few years I've had the chance to run physical game sessions and workshops in a variety of settings around Europe and to co-organize a monthly physical game meetup of my own in Berlin while I was living there. For me, the biggest challenge in all these games is the very first step of getting people to feel comfortable enough to ignore whatever fears or misgivings they might have and make the personal choice to play. Once people decide for themselves to go for it, all sorts of fun become possible, but getting past that first step can be tough.

I think Bernie captured why this is so hard (and why it's so much fun when it happens) when he wrote in *The Playful Path*,

"A playful path must ultimately take you beyond remembered things, beyond the familiar, the recognizable . . . It's mystery not mastery that brings people together." Play is an exploration of the unknown, so it's no wonder that even the most simple physical game can be intimidating.

This venture into the unknown is something I explored in my game *Surrender*, developed in 2015 with Sarah Homewood, Johannes Følsgaard, and Olli Harjola at Lyst Summit, a conference and game jam about love, sex, and romance in games. *Surrender* is played by three people: a "Sensor" who stands in the middle and closes their eyes, and two "Pleasers" who stand on either side of the Sensor. The Pleasers have one minute to touch the hands and forearms of the Sensor using their own hands and forearms, and the Sensor takes steps in the direction of whichever sensation they find most pleasing. The Pleaser whose side the Sensor ends up on after the round is over "wins."

I originally saw *Surrender* as sharply separate from the more light-hearted games I usually play, but I think the challenges involved in running it are a direct extension of those inherent in all physical games. Setting the right tone is always important, and most physical games involve some degree of being vulnerable and intimate with others. Many games also involve learning about yourself and others in unexpected ways in the course of playing. And in all types of physical games, there's just something about this process of being vulnerable and learning together that forms deep bonds among the players.

I think this is key to the idea of the "play community" that Bernie so often discussed. "Play isn't ours to create," he wrote, "it's ours to discover." Something about discovering play brings people together and connects them, and, when you think about it, seeing the unknown and unfamiliar as fun instead of scary is kind of revolutionary. Bernie often advised me to focus on the fun, and I'm starting to think that maybe this is what he was getting at.

PLAY SETS US FREE!
STEPHEN CONWAY

When we play together, we are connected by the invisible thread of playfulness. This relationship—not you or me—but us, together, playing, creates a space for us in that moment that neither of us could forge on our own. We are free in that moment, liberated by each other. And we might find ourselves thinking or feeling or doing things that seem way beyond our abilities when we're alone.

Bernie called this coliberation.

We see it in sports. Teammates totally in sync with each other suddenly rising up together and beginning to perform on a level that seems almost superhuman.

We see it at the theater or a symphony with everyone on stage playing as a collective whole—a moment of perfect harmony. That pure sweet sound is impossible to forget.

But we don't have to be able to dunk a ball or play an amazing trumpet to experience coliberation. And it doesn't need a crowd.

It's a moment of freedom and awareness that can flash into existence any time you make the choice to play.

Play is a lifelong choice available to us all. And when you play, you help set yourself and others free.

There's a simple, beautiful idea that Bernie and I each found, like a shiny rock on the beach.

Playfulness is a posture, not a pose, a stance that you can take—or a set of lenses that help you see the world in a new light throughout the journey of your life. It's a choice we can make—to be playful, to find joy in the everyday, in each other, in the community, in art and science, in the world in all its vast possibilities.

It can start at the game table for many. Giving ourselves permission to play, to find that sense of freedom and joy—the feeling of challenge and risk and reward that can only come from a well-played game.

That playful spirit is what brings us back to games as adults. Rediscovering something, unlocking something that was always already there.

The leap that Bernie made and that I am still making is that you can take that spirit with you beyond games. Any path you walk in life can be a playful path, *your* playful path.

You can choose to play, to have fun, to find joy, and that choice is one that comes from a place of profound imagination, courage, and freedom.

We even have the freedom and power to change the rules. To make things more inclusive, to make the game more challenging and more fun.

Playfulness is profound but, when expressed, it should be profoundly silly.

Take a beat, find the fun when and where you can in life. Take life just seriously enough that you figure out how to play with it.

Choosing to play bucks so much of what we are taught to believe is important or vital for being successful. And yet, choosing to play brings us closer to contentment.

Choosing to play makes us lighter, freer, brings us closer to knowing ourselves and others.

Choosing to play allows us to savor moments and memories with those we love, or with complete strangers.

Put simply, play can transform us into better versions of ourselves.

COME OUT & PLAY

CATHERINE HERDLICK

When I moved to San Francisco several years ago, I brought along with me the physical games festival Come Out & Play. It was exciting to curate and run the festival in San Francisco, the birthplace of the New Games movement, Burning Man, and so many other feats of collective creativity.

At its height in 2012, Come Out & Play SF ran for a month and was headquartered at SOMArts, a cultural center whose mission includes "fostering access to arts and culture for collective liberation and self-determination." The huge main gallery presented a unique curatorial opportunity for self-directed play. To supplement the original games we curated, we painted an infinite hopscotch court on the floor, hung a colorful ten-foot-tall grid of dots for giant games of *Dots and Boxes*, and set out a supersized variant of magnetic poetry (stacks of paper with letters on them and rolls of blue painter's tape) on white pedestals. The message was clear: THIS IS YOUR PLAYSPACE. The crowd during opening night was electric and inspired: people climbed on each other's shoulders to reach the highest rows of *Dots and Boxes*, drew distinctive "tags" to claim boxes, nested tiny games within a single box, Sharpied everything, used the blue tape to create elaborate murals and games of hangman on the blank walls, and even used the tape to decorate themselves. Bouncy balls came out of nowhere. Elderly people in suits and sweater sets hopscotched along throughout the chaos, creating house rules along their way. The distinction between players and designers eroded quickly, as I'd hoped it would.

In the smaller back gallery of SOMArts, my husband, Gabe Smedresmen, had installed *The Hearst Collection*, a game that challenged players to steal a work of art from the back wall without triggering the laser security system. This ironic piece, polished and ambitious in its build-out, tested the patience of the team at SOMArts, but in the end they loved it because it drew massive crowds. *The Hearst Collection* was an iteration of *The Bellagio Heist*, an interactive installation Gabe and I had created and run together out of our apartment in Haight-Ashbury on Halloween weekend in 2010 as part of the annual citywide game *Journey to the End of the Night*. That night, the San Francisco Fire Department was summoned by our building's fire alarm system twice due to our fog machines. Rather than shut us down (and disappoint the hundreds of people waiting to maneuver through the laser maze), the firefighters suggested we use dry ice next time and took advantage of their authority only to cut the line to try out the laser maze themselves.

SOMArts's willingness to surrender its pristine galleries to mischief, SFFD's subtle nod of approval, and thousands of players' joy at subverting expectations (of a game, a gallery, and the city) are testament to our collective ability to redistribute power through trust, reciprocity, and imagination. Such redistribution is a constant social need, and it is why I coach students and collaborators to welcome rule-bending, to design for cheaters, and to let go of trying to control everything.

THE WORKING IMAGINATION

I've convinced you, I hope, that coliberation—that imagining together—can be freeing and satisfying and revelatory and bring closeness and discoveries about each other and about yourself. Which is all very well and good. If that was all that coliberating did, it would still be enough.

But there is more to it than this.

Coliberation is one of the ways that we make together, make freely and fun-ly—and if we cultivate coliberation in ourselves and our relationships, we can find in it a source of being together, together.

I did say, way back at the beginning of the book, that this was a vocational course. A university, even.

So in this chapter of the book I want to talk about how coliberation and imagination can play out in all different areas of our lives—how they can help us to create and to act together, in science, in business, in art, anywhere we might want to create—and especially anywhere we might want to create together.

But because I'm me, let's start with talking about another game.

SOMETHING TO PLAY: *SINGING BLATHER*

You probably won't be surprised, given the nature of the *Blather* games, that there's a chorale-type version where everybody (as many bodies as you can get together) sings together the same tune at the same time—except, like in all versions of *Blather*, each singer sings whatever words seem to be songworthy.

It helps if you all pick the same tune. Any tune to anything everyone knows: "Twinkle, Twinkle, Little Star," for example. Or perhaps "Baa, Baa, Black Sheep," or even "The Alphabet Song." (Okay, so they're all the same tune. You could try maybe a birthday song or, if you're of the right age, "Sixteen Tons.")

Anyhow, the idea here is to pick one tune. And start singing the tune at the same time. The lyrics you make up as you go along. Without stopping to think.

Singing Blather may seem like one small step from ordinary *Blather*, but it turns out to be a quantum leap for all blathering-kind.

Imagine that you're blathering to the tune of "Row Row Row Your Boat." With, let's say, three people. It might go something like this:

Hello, this is fun, at least I hope it is, because it makes me so confused I don't know what to sing	Hi, there, we played before, I think I remember your name, yes this game is really fun and I'm just as confused as you	Hey you two, I remember you, but I forget both your names, my name is Fred so what are yours tell me when you can

And, should you choose to go to the conceptual beyond, you could try singing in rounds.

You're singing, and creating, and talking, and listening, and blathering—all at once, together.

DAYDREAMS AND DOODLES

If you think about the sort of mood that you would need to be in to play *Singing Blather*, or the sort of mood that *Singing Blather* might help you get into, then you may start to see the sort of mood that we need in order to create, and especially to create together.

Let's say we want to draw something, or paint something, or write a poem or a book, or sculpt something, or find a new answer for something that's been bothering us, or come up with a joke or a slogan, or make a game or a plan. There's a state of mind that we need to get into first.

Let's call it "play mind."

There we can almost forget about what we're "really" trying to do, and just fool around with ideas and stuff. Toy with them. Close our eyes, maybe, and imagine them looking or sounding or feeling like this, or like that, or going together or hanging from each other. Even before we start making notes or sketches or outlines or drafts.

We tell our inner judges and critics and analysts to take a proverbial hike. We need them out of the building, somewhere far away, so we can fool around, toy with images and ideas, drop them from our imaginary towers and see how they bounce, launch them and see how they fly, shake them up and see how we can make them fit together.

It's a time for doodles and daydreams, for imagining, for playing around. A time for getting into that state of mind where everything is very, very much like play, like what we do when we're doing something just for the fun of it.

It's a very delicate state of mind, this playing-around state. It's hard to explain, almost impossible to excuse, even to ourselves. It's really, truly the fun part—the part that makes us actually want to do all this thinking and inventing and creating and imagining we so much love to do.

But there are pressures. Deadlines. There are people who need us to come up with something final, something they can sell or build or hang on a wall. We are obliged to produce, to look like we're working.

And yet, we have to shut all that out and make ourselves play anyway. Not work. Play.

This shutting ourselves away from all things purposeful and giving ourselves permission to play, this understanding, this ability, this discipline that we have developed to let ourselves go to that place of doodles and daydreams and have fun despite all else, this enforced suspension of worry, of purpose: this is the art and heart of the creative act.

SOMETHING TO PLAY: *DRAWING TOGETHER*

This next game was sent to me by Rick Hamrick. I took the liberty of giving it a name. It's a game that involves making something together—and it uses this "play mind" of creating, and not thinking too hard about it, that so many of these creative games help us access.

The game is simple: start with a blank piece of paper on a flat surface. Two people sit at opposite sides of the paper. Each is given a pen and instructed to start drawing a picture on the half of the page closest to them. Each person is to draw only on their side. The challenge is to adjust the image you are seeking to create so that it is complemented somehow by the image the other person is creating on the other half of the piece of paper.

So, of course, each player is seeking to incorporate the other's art even as it is being created. A moving target!

Only one rule: no talking about the art in progress. Conversation is welcome, but it cannot be about the game or what each is drawing.

When one of the two players decides that the work is done, the other person has a brief time to complete the bit they are drawing, and then the game concludes with each person describing their work. An added twist would be for each to guess what the other had in mind prior to the person's describing it. The emphasis is on how each incorporated the other person's work into their own and telling a good story about it.

No winner or loser, only time spent in a cooperative task where cooperation is made a challenge because you cannot talk about it. And the storytelling part at the end can be outrageous and laughter inducing.

I see many implications. Many applications. Many variations—like with *Blather*, we can imagine so many different variations and ways to play and make together.

Of course, creativity and imagination are not the same thing. Everything I've learned about imagination over the last very many years is based on this simple observation. Though they frequently call on each other, they are different. And in probing that difference lies a much clearer understanding of what imagination is all about.

Here's an explication of that difference from a book by Ann Pendleton-Jullian and John Seely Brown called *Pragmatic Imagination*:

> Creative activity aims to do something purposeful. The imagination is something that emerges. While creativity works towards products that exist in the real world and have real-world purpose, the product of the imagination is the "imagined object"; it is the image itself.
>
> . . . It is precisely because the imagination is given permission to play without pragmatic intent that it finds connections between things that are not obvious or easy. It finds correspondences that the reasoning mind might never see. It plays with boundaries. It lets thoughts and partial thoughts jump fences. While not purposeful by intent, or pragmatic by nature, it is precisely this kind of activity that has a pragmatic possibility in a world that is rapidly changing and radically contingent.

Later on in the book, the authors make a useful distinction between "experimental imagination" (like Einstein's gedanken-experiments) and "free play imagination":

> The free play imagination does not subscribe to the boundaries of what one knows, or knows how to do. It is serendipitous, intuitive, and completely at home not knowing why it sees what it sees. This

is the imagination that we most often associate with the realm of the unconscious mind, which "runs in the background" during waking hours and dominates our dreaming . . . What distinguishes the imagination of free play from the experimental imagination is its motivation. The experimental imagination starts with the question and/or an individual's creative practice and history. These serve as its center of gravity. Whether to make music, experiment with gestures and color on canvas, wrestle with string theory, the experimental imagination honors this search. It is focused play.

This is my kind of imagination. My kind of play. A kind of play in which I can get totally and deliciously lost. Creativity of the purposeless kind. Imagination for the fun of it. But just because play and imagination may not be motivated by a question doesn't mean that they might not sometimes come up with answers.

MAKING IMAGINATION REAL

Lev Vygotsky, in his "Imagination and Creativity in Childhood," also talks about the "creative imagination." Though his professional focus is clearly on children and childhood, he has a lot to say about the creative imagination in adults as well.

In the beginning of the essay, he describes the connection between imagination and experience. He makes the simultaneously obvious and profound observation that because experience is the very stuff of imagination, the older we get (and the more experience we acquire), the richer the imagination. Imagination is a gift. And the depth of the imagination is the gift of aging:

> the creative activity of the imagination depends directly on the richness and variety of a person's previous experience because this

experience provides the material from which the products of fantasy are constructed. The richer a person's experience, the richer is the material his imagination has access to. This is why a child has a less rich imagination than an adult, because his experience has not been as rich.

He goes on to describe how the creative imagination, though based on experience (and memory), creates something new—something more than a replay of the experience on which it is based, a transformation of memories into a newly imagined experience.

Next, Vygotsky notes that even when we are experiencing something that is pretended (a work of art, of fiction, or of our own unaided minds), the emotions produced in us are real. This is a powerful insight, creating a connection between the actual and the imaginary, and helping to establish imagination as something central to the arts and to our emotional lives.

When he goes into his room in the half dark, a child may have the illusion that clothes hanging up are a strange man or a robber who has broken into his house. The image of the robber, created by the child's imagination, is not real, but the fear and terror the child experiences are completely real, the child's true experience. Something similar happens with every real construct of fantasy and it is this psychological law that should explain to us why works of art created by their authors' imaginations can have such a strong emotional effect on us.

The passions and fates of imaginary characters, their joys and sorrows move, disturb, and excite us, despite the fact that we know these are not real events, but rather the products of fantasy. This occurs only because the emotions that take hold of us from the artistic images on the pages of books or from the stage are completely real and we experience them truly, seriously, and deeply.

And then Vygotsky establishes the deep connection between reality and the imagination, showing how imagination is not only based on reality but actually leads to the creation of a new reality.

> . . . a construct of fantasy may represent something substantially new, never encountered before in human experience and without correspondence to any object that actually exists in reality; however, once it has been externally embodied, that is, has been given material form, this crystallized imagination that has become an object begins to actually exist in the real world, to affect other things.
>
> In this way imagination becomes reality. Examples of such crystallized or embodied imagination include any technical device, machine, or instrument. These were created by the combinatory imagination of human beings and do not correspond to any model existing in reality, but they have the most persuasive, active, and practical association with reality in that once they have been given material form, they become just as real as other things and affect the surrounding real environment.

And finally, he zooms further back to give us a new perspective on human consciousness, noting that the interaction between the imagined and the created world becomes its own phenomenon—a never-ending cycle in which each contributes to the evolution of the other.

Beautiful, no?

So we understand that creativity and imagination are not the same thing—but they go together, one linked with another, and imagination can be a creative act.

SOMETHING TO PLAY: *FOLEY A CAPELLA*

A Foley artist is someone who reproduces everyday sounds and creates the sound effects that movies and television shows might have in them. The squelching of feet in mud, the smashing of a safe through a window, the click of a lock, the swoosh of a cape, the tiny, quick footsteps of a sausage dog trying to keep up.

Foley a Capella, as you might have guessed, is about making sound effects using only your voice and whatever other sound-making affordances that your body is heir to (hand-clapping, finger-snapping, tongue-clicking . . .).

And, in this instance, it's also about using those effects to accompany an imaginary movie that is being imaginarily filmed.

The script? There are two ways to do this (at least):

In one version of the game, the group decides on a story everyone knows (Peter Pan? Pinocchio? Perhaps Jack and Jill?) and imagines the film running without sound, collectively Foleyizing it into the shared reality.

In another, the movie is being imaginarily written, one word or phrase or line at a time. The writers? Everyone who imagines themselves such. The Foley-makers? Foleying along as so inspired. For example:

"In jumps Jiminy Cricket . . ."
("Boing! Chirp!")
"Pinocchio is so excited to see his best friend that he starts
    dancing."
(Foley artist clatters his feet on the ground.)

Any Foley-maker can become a writer when they aren't Foleying around, and vice versa.

IMAGINATION AND SCIENCE

It's not just what we traditionally think of as "creative" fields that require imagination.

I'd like to talk for a moment about Richard Feynman. Feynman was a Nobel laureate for his contributions to theoretical physics. For me, however, it was his contributions to our understanding of both imagination and fun that are the most noteworthy of all his many accomplishments. Here's an excerpt from Feynman's 1983 BBC Broadcast entitled "Fun to Imagine":

> It's interesting that some people find science so easy, and others find it kind of dull and difficult, especially kids; you know, some of them are just heated up, and I don't know why it is. It's the same for all [people]. For instance some people love music and I could never carry a tune. I lose a great deal of pleasure out of that and I think that people lose a lot of pleasure who find science dull. In the case of science, I think that one of the things that makes it difficult is that it takes a lot of imagination. It's very hard to imagine all the crazy things that things really are like.

So, it's not so much all the formulas and strange mathematics and convoluted reasoning and complex charts and arcane language. It's that a lot of things science seems to be about are just plain hard to imagine. And yet imagination is key to scientific understanding.

And all of a sudden, Feynman is talking not just about the physics of it all but about the aesthetics, the sheer beauty, because that's what he sees when he imagines, for example, how atoms move:

> I find myself trying to imagine all kinds of things all the time, and I get a kick out of it, like a runner gets a kick out of sweating. I

GET A KICK out of thinking about these things. I can't stop. I can talk forever!

And it's not just Feynman.

The continued evolution of theoretical physics, especially when exploring the strange realities of the quantum world, has led to profound discoveries about the nature of the universe and our very bodies, and to even more profound discoveries about things like imagination and the truth of beauty. In an all-too-brief 2013 article from the BBC entitled "Why Science Needs Imagination and Beauty," we can read the following words from another Nobel Prize recipient, Frank Wilczek:

> Not many people truly appreciate what happened in physics in the last part of the 20th Century. We understood at a level whose profundity would be difficult to exaggerate what matter is. We really have the equations for the different fundamental building blocks of matter—the different particles have mathematical characterizations that are precise and elegant. They have no secrets. In principle we have the equations.
>
> The bad news, however, is we are not so good at solving them. There are still gaps in fundamental understanding, we have very good equations or practical purposes, but they are kind of lopsided; they are beautiful but not quite as beautiful as they should be given they are close to God's last word in some sense. We're trying to think of better ways to solve the equations, which takes a lot of imagination because they describe an unfamiliar world—it's a very small world and things behave differently in it. The only way to get experience is to play around with the equations and imagine how they might behave in different circumstances, it's more like imaginative play than anything else.

The laws we have discovered, especially in the quantum world, are so strange you have to play with them in your mind. Usually what you envision is wrong, but it's mind expanding and every once in a while you see something that may be right. Sometimes it even is right.

Virtual legions of theoretical physicists have shown over and over again that, aided by nothing more than imagination, research, and intense curiosity, we can imagine the entire universe into being.

Of course, we don't have to limit these cosmic powers to physicists. Science fiction writers, poets, novelists, teachers, theologians, architects, engineers, economists, city planners, politicians, and playwrights all have, by virtue of their imaginations, contributed to weaving the very fabric of our collective reality.

Of course, there is a distinction to be made here. Physicists, for example, contribute to a different aspect of our reality than, for another example, fiction writers. When physicists make an assumption, like the universe being a hologram, they know they can't prove it, but they can assume it and see what happens as a result. Fiction writers like to assume things and then pretend those things are real. Both connect to us through the imagination, but one must, out of the necessity of their mission, substantiate their work through their understanding and the observations of their peers; the others, the artists and planners and politicians, are not so much into substantiation as they are into becoming part of a shared belief, a community of believers, one might say.

These callings are not the same. But they all depend on imagination.

STRENGTHENING THE GROUP IMAGINATION

To make the shared imagination a more enduring faculty of any group, it is only necessary to lead the group in a varied enough collection of experiences that challenge the imagination in different ways.

Just like you can strengthen your own imagination by imagining and by noticing when the opportunities to imagine arise, so you can strengthen the collective imagination of a group that works together by giving them opportunities to practice and teaching them to look out for moments to imagine together.

This is not a surprising truth. We get better at imagination by imagining. And we get better at imagining with other people by, well, imagining with other people.

We can see this is true when we look at the most imaginative of us. Let us take for a moment the idea of a "paracosm," a detailed imaginary world created inside someone's mind. Or, of course, as we know so well by now, it can also be created inside two minds. And, as we know equally well, a paracosm shared is even more paracosmic than a paracosm of your own.

If we look at that definition, "a detailed imaginary world created inside someone's mind," the key words are "detailed," "imaginary," and "mind": "Mind" because that's where the whole thing takes place—there's nothing else needed, just a mind. "Imaginary" because that's what this whole magical gift, this amazing faculty of mind that we falsely attribute only to children and artists, is called. And "detailed" because that's where the amazement lives—that we can create complex, interrelated, lifelike images that live and interact according to their own laws.

WHY IMAGINE?

Clive Thompson's 2012 *Wired* article "Clive Thompson on the Importance of Fan Fiction" updates the concept of paracosm perfectly. He not only writes about the increasing popularity of fan fiction, but also underlines its relevance to children's creative lives:

> You could, as many do, cluck disapprovingly at this activity. Haven't these folks got anything better to do with their time?
>
> To which I reply: No, they don't. Because they're creating paracosms—an activity that, research is showing, builds creative skills that pay off in real life.
>
> Paracosms are the fantasy worlds that many dreamy, imaginative kids like to invent when they're young. Some of history's most creative adults had engaged in "worldplay" as children. The Brontë siblings, in one famous example, concocted paracosms so elaborate that they documented them with meticulous maps, drawings, and hundreds of pages of encyclopedic writing.

And he continues:

> It now appears that, like the Brontës, kids who engage in paracosmic play are more likely to be creative as adults.

Thus, I comment:

"Ah and aha," we can sigh, smilingly. We need not only learn about the fan fiction fenom but also both encourage and support our teens in their efforts on behalf thereof. So they'll grow up more creative, don't you know.

And now I muse and opine:

Of course, why should we need the excuses? Let them have fun imagining their worlds so they'll be creative when they grow up? I mean, what are they already when they're imagining worlds?

Oh, having fun.

How lovably childish.

In fact (tongue not in cheek), they are demonstrating not only their creativity but their abilities to use their imaginations to maintain and develop an increasingly complex and detailed world: envisioning characters and costumes, landscapes and architecture, cities and societies. Day after day, sometimes year after year, a city, world, solar system, or cosmos of their own making—an almost tangibly imagined and often shared space that is both nonexistent and totally engaging.

Yes, they are playing. Yes, they are doing it all because they think it's fun. And all we have to do is respect their genius and walk away. Or play with them, if they let us. And be reminded that we also have such powers, such gifts, and that they are deeply fun. Maybe we can get other people to join us, for the fun of it, so to speak.

Thompson is enlightened enough to recognize that for the majority of adults, fun isn't enough. Imagination has to have *purpose* to be of any value to us at all. So he concludes with yet another powerful observation: "The future belongs to those who can imagine it."

And that, more or less, is what I've been saying, or seeing, in this whole imaginary enterprise of mine. That's the promise of the premise. And if we can somehow contribute to (or learn from) our children's abilities to imagine a better future (with something like, maybe, world peace—all right, maybe not world—how about family), they will manage to build themselves a better one.

We don't need to be Brontës to construct our own imaginary world and to get fun and fulfillment and discovery from it. But then, if the Brontës hadn't made up their own worlds, separately and together, then perhaps they wouldn't have ended up being the Brontës either.

SOMETHING TO PLAY: *THE LABEL GAME*

This next game is a game about imagining yourself, and different versions of yourself. We've talked before about how whenever we imagine someone else, they're just another aspect of ourselves. Well, this time, we take that other aspect of ourselves out for a walk to meet other aspects of other people's selves.

You know those tags and badges you get at parties or conferences—those things you write your name on and then stick on yourself or hang around your neck? Name tags, I think, is what you call them.

That's what you need to play *The Label Game*—say, maybe three per player. They're like five dollars for a hundred. You can probably find them at most any office supply store.

So, you get a bunch of them and enough markers so that you're not going to worry about people not having several to use. And, as people come in, you ask them to make a label for themselves.

You might have a list of label ideas handy just to get things started, like:

1 Percenter, All Powerful, Arch Nemesis of Evil, Bipartisan, Bisexual, Buff, Curiously Loving Sadist, Devastatingly Handsome, Devious, Emotionally Unstable, Fabulous, Famous, Fashionable, Fool, Gnarly, Hard of Hearing, Holier than Thou, Holy One, Homeless, Horny, Hug-Deprived, Impressionable, Inarticulate, Inebriated, Influential, Intellectual, Invisible, Lord of All Creation, Magician, Naive, Naked, Nobel Laureate, Not Who I Appear to Be, Over Protective,

Pole Dancer, Prophet, Queer, Sexy, Shaman, Shawoman, Stunning, Sweet-Smelling, Too Marvelous for Words, Unlabeled, Vastly Superior, Ventriloquist, Wealthy, Wicked, Wise, Witch, Your Grace, Your Highness, Your Holiness, Your Honor, Your Mamma.

They can use another badge for their name if they so wish. Or not if they don't. They can have as many badges as they want—though three is the recommended maximum.

After they are all properly enbadged, they spend the next fifteen or so minutes people-mixing, as if they were in some kind of cocktail party, treating each other according to their label. So, should you have a label that says "Innocent," everyone would respond to whatever you said to them as if it were coming from an innocent person.

That's pretty much the whole game. You might spend some of the time looking for someone with a label you especially want to spend time with. Or looking for several people whose labels would make them want to spend time with you. You might enjoy introducing people to each other in a host-like manner.

You might want to change your label, add another label, or trade labels with someone else. You might want to remove all your labels and walk around unlabeled. You might want to sit somewhere and just watch. And whatever you do, whomever you encounter, your only goal is to help people feel that they are precisely and entirely as labeled.

It's kind of a socially aware game, where you think about how we label people. Except it's different because we're labeling ourselves. And that little difference is part of what makes the whole thing so much fun. (Another part of course is just walking around being treated as if you were invisible, naked, and/or fabulously wealthy—depending on which labels you've picked.)

We might expect children to imagine. We might even expect people involved in art and writing to value their imaginations. When we've thought about it a little we might not be surprised to find that imagination has a home in science as well.

But one of the things I've found most heartening in recent times is that people have begun to talk about how play and imagination have a home even in business, in meetings, in worlds where we might not expect to find them. Let's take a look at the "playfulness" card from the Group Works deck, a deck of cards that is intended to help people run meetings and group sessions—by identifying and inspiring positive patterns of behavior.

The Group Works deck was created as a collaborative effort by the Group Pattern Language Project. The deck has almost a hundred cards on nifty subjects like "purpose" and "moving into alignment." The playfulness card reads:

> Invite light-hearted and high-spirited interaction to exercise mind, senses, imagination and body, to engender creativity, and deepen relationships. Playfulness may be evoked through structured but fun ways to engage relevant topics, or restorative breaks that allow laughter free reign, or may simply show up as humor.

The Group Pattern Language Project discusses play as a "purposeful enjoyable activity" and talks about the role it can play in group processes. It can help people learn, the group says; it can create memorable experiences; it can help us access a different part of ourselves; it can free a group from inhibitions and bring it together and disrupt ingrained power dynamics.

The playfulness card is a wise and reassuring card, and all the more so for coming from this context where we might not expect imagination and play to find a home. It is wise in that it invites play into the heart of the business environment. It is reassuring for the same reason.

It talks about being "light-hearted." Yes, yes. One of my favorite phrases. Light, as in the light that lights the heart and the world. Light, as in unencumbered, weightless, free.

The card goes on to describe a list of similarly wise "caveats" because for people to accept the invitation to play they need certain reassurances. Though this is especially obvious in the business environment, it is equally true anywhere.

Here's that list:

- Trust is prerequisite
- The group needs to believe this is a good use of their time
- The activity needs to be relevant to the purpose of the group process (and also needs a debrief to articulate and reaffirm this)
- There needs to be a teachable moment and/or relationship-building outcome
- Beware of the influence of alcohol on games/play activities—too much lack of inhibition can be a liability or personal safety issue
- Some people will be inhibited or embarrassed by play, so you need to be alert to make sure this doesn't occur

Of course, this is for meetings. In a more public setting, one in which the invitation to play is just that—an invitation, and the agenda is obviously devoted to having fun together—the caveats are fewer and more easily addressed.

Trust is engendered by making sure that people know that their acceptance of the invitation to play is totally voluntary.

That not-playing is as valid a response to the invitation as playing is.

The belief that this is a good use of time is reinforced by the fun they are having.

The relevance is to the individual and collective desire to have fun. No further explanation needed.

The teachable moment and/or relationship-building outcome is self-evident every moment of every game.

People who feel the least bit embarrassed or inhibited are free to quit whenever and join whenever. This is the way it works in public play. The freedom to quit, the permission to join is all that is needed to make an invitation to play the invitation that it is meant to be.

It's so heartening to find that some of the things we learn when we approach play as an end in itself are the same as the things that people find out when they think about play as a way of co-creation and collaboration, to see people approaching the business of meetings, and the meeting of businesses, and find that they are thinking about playfulness and the depth that playfulness can bring to the process of being and thinking and talking together.

SOMETHING TO PLAY: *THE ORCHESTRA GAME*

To start this game, we need to first assemble the orchestra. This is a little like the game we talked about early on from Augusto Boal's collection, *The Orchestra and the Conductor*, but because we are further along in the book we can maybe get away without quite so many rules, not absolutely as many structures. We've learned, perhaps, that rules are there to help us to play, and if we don't need them, we can change or discard them as we like.

So, an orchestra.

Let's say there are strings, winds, brass, and percussion. We could also say there is only percussion, or strings, or brass, if that's what we wanted to say. Or we could also say that in addition to strings, winds, brass, and percussion, we have voice. And some voices hum, and some mumble, and some sing. It all depends on the size of the group, the level of seriousness, and the piece people seem to want to perform or make up. "Row, Row, Row Your Boat" is always a good choice, as is the fourth movement of Beethoven's Ninth. If some people are less than eager to perform, they may also designate themselves as "enthusiastic audience."

Next, everyone selects an instrument, closes their eyes, and starts playing. Closing their eyes is important! After a brief, cacophonic whine, with their eyes still closed, people assemble into groups of similar instruments, assuming an orchestra-like array. Of course, with their eyes closed, this is a challenge. They will have to listen very carefully.

And when they feel sufficiently assembled, still with their eyes closed, everyone "tunes-up" until they reach a chord.

The final movement of the game begins with the opening of the eyes, which is always amusing.

And then, without further ado or adieu, the performance.

After their performance, the players take their bows. First, of course, the conductor. Then, at the direction of the conductor, the soloists, the choir, and, finally, the different segments of the orchestra. If there is no audience, they bow to each other.

Finally, if so moved, without discussion or elaboration, they perform an encore as if they already knew exactly what piece they had planned to play. If it doesn't quite work like that in practice—well, no matter.

ENTER THE DRAGON

MARY FLANAGAN

RAAAWWRRRR!!!!!! In one memorable conference workshop with Bernie De Koven in the Netherlands a few years back, a group of game designers and scholars gathered for a play workshop with the one and only BDK.

Those who came were quite game, so to speak. One exercise/game that we played with embodiment and imagination consisted of acting out two animal imitations: The player who is "it" stands in the middle of the circle of players and points to someone while calling out either "elephant" or "giraffe." The person pointed at forms the center of a three-person creature and either raises their arms to make the tall neck of the giraffe, with the surrounding players on the left and right making the body, or the center person forms the elephant by making the head and trunk. The trick is for the person who is "it" to choose clusters around the circle who might be distracted, leading those without razor sharp playground skills to form the wrong animal or join the wrong group under the intense heat of the pretend sun.

After a round, I shouted out a third animal to try: a "dragon." A group started experimenting with a dragon head—how to make jaws and mimic fiery breath. This iterative process took mere seconds. Players act spontaneously when fully engaged, when the imagination unleashes, when there is no fear of judgment or penalty. The dragon worked, and successful dragon heads triggered impromptu long-tail dragon dances around the circle.

Just being around Bernie made for an automatic safe space by his very force of nature, where peers—who might have been reticent, or critical, or judgmental of their own performance or the performance of others—leapt into play with abandon. This is the role that imagination plays: we invent "dragons" when we're not afraid to leap off the creative cliff into the unknown. As we play deeply, we become absorbed in the precious present moment given to us. We can't worry about the past. We can't predict the future. We just are, in the here and now. It's similar to gratitude. You live it. It's all encompassing.

The spirit of play embodies freedom, choice, and lightness. Imagination expands fundamental possibilities. Pure imaginative play starts off as one thing and can shift in a new direction like the wind. Such play is wild, free, and unfettered. It pokes fun at itself and offers an affectionate guffaw at the absurdity of life as we know it. This lightness and freedom is what Buddhist monks aim for as an optimal way of being in the world. Even the Dalai Lama, in a CNN interview, said "Thinking only of the negative aspect doesn't help to find solutions and it destroys peace of mind . . . I love smiles, and my wish is to see more smiles, real smiles . . . If we want those smiles, we must create the reasons that make them appear" (Christensen 2017). Play is a fundamental part of the human spirit. Surprisingly, such freedom does not always sit well with people, even designers. But for me, imaginative play sings into my cells.

Another game Bernie had us play back in 2011 was a blind-folded touching game, *Prui*. I don't remember the details, but I remember the thought "this is so hippie" passing through my mind. The game involved touching people around you, and sometimes, well, feeling up said random people. Hey, we were blindfolded! For a moment I thought we were simulating a free love social experiment for some 1960s movie. But imaginative play tolerates no judgment or it ceases, so I had to drop all my preconceptions. And instead of being suggestive or lewd, the game seemed to bring players to a state of innocence and trust that I've never before or since seen at a conference. There we were, players, surrounded by the simplicity of connection with the mysterious realization of sensory deprivation. I remember feeling that the sense of trust that emerged was fundamental, like that of an infant holding on to a father's wide fingers for the very first time.

Each time we play deeply, we transport ourselves to some new or beautiful part of ourselves. We allow ourselves to go to unfamiliar places. We expand the very nature of who we are.

Bernie has guided many a soul to reach back and rescue these lost core selves. Players become as open and as imaginative as the fantastic shapes of clouds making infinite heavens. Play is a vital way in which we connect with each other and the world around us. If we can just grab on to this open and wild and trusting spirit, the world will indeed be better off. The imaginative spirit is not something that can be taught, exactly, but it can be acknowledged, nurtured, and allowed to flourish. It's the core of being alive, the foundation of optimism and possibility.

In the coming years, the planet will face unprecedented speeds of change and challenge. We'll need this spirit to fuel the hard decisions and actions to come. We'll need to find surprising answers that only free, wild, and beautiful play can bring to us. In fact, we'll need to rely on our imaginative spirit in order to thrive. So get ready—you'll likely be summoning the silliness nurtured by BDK on a daily basis.

The event described here happened at Think Design Play, the fifth DiGRA conference hosted by Utrecht School of the Arts in November 2011.

COLIBERATION
DOUGLAS WILSON

Bernie's notion of "coliberation" is sometimes explained as a sweet spot between "me" and "we"—a balancing of the needs of the individual and the collective to help players avoid the twin dangers of alienation and conformity. That's partially correct, but I suspect Bernie's play on words is aimed at articulating something even greater—something beyond a point on a linear continuum, something more transcendent. Coliberation suggests a kind of social magic.

Back in my college days, a group of my friends became obsessed with the classic parlor game *Mafia* (also known as *Werewolf*). *Mafia* is a party game about psychology and paranoia. The basic idea is that a few chosen liars (the mafia) secretly work together against the collective interests of the majority (the citizens). Players, assigned hidden roles, sit in a circle and dish out mob justice (or, frequently, injustice) as they try to deduce who is on the mafia team. No dice, no cards, no board, just accusations, arguments, and votes.

One of our regulars was my friend Josh, infamous for his maddeningly unpredictable style of play. The thing I remember most is how he would frequently lie about what role he had in ways you might not expect. For example, as a citizen player he might falsely claim that he had been dealt the special sheriff role . . . effectively undermining the real sheriff *on his own team.*

To be clear, there are certainly tactical reasons why a player, even a member of the citizen team, might want to lie about their role. But in the case of Josh's antics, I don't think "strategy" was ever a major consideration. In fact, his lies would frequently doom his team to an insurmountable amount of confusion. As I understand it, Josh was primarily trying to mess with us, and, in the process, produce something unexpected—something we might remember.

Well, he certainly succeeded. More than a decade later, I still remember how, in the aftermath of those games, Josh's face would finally break into a big knowing smile as he fessed up to his ill-judged schemes.

What strikes me about Josh is that he was simultaneously a spoilsport *and* a source of collective inspiration. Sure, Josh's antics might have torpedoed some games for his team, but they also served to remind us that *Mafia* could be about more than just strategy. For us, the game became an arena to out-impress each other, to craft the perfect lie, to make the funniest argument. Memorable performers like Josh pushed us to become loose cannons, all of us.

Reflecting on what I've learned from both Bernie and Josh, I'd argue that coliberation is something more than a mathematical trade-off, something richer than a compromise between two options. The magic of coliberation is that it is "me" and "we" *at the same time*, a kind of quantum social physics that allows for selfishness and selflessness simultaneously.

This simultaneity is what I cherish most about games, and it's something I hope we take to heart, both when we play games and when we make them . . . and when we blur that distinction.

LIKE MANY OF MY GENERATION

AKIRA THOMPSON

Like many of my generation, my first exposure to Bernie's work was through many of the New Games—played with parachutes, giant balls, or no equipment at all—that I played during physical education classes in grade school. At the time, of course, I had no idea that these games were designed with a particular philosophy in mind. I only understood that my classmates and I had fun playing them.

It wasn't until much later in life when I wanted nothing more than to become a game designer that I read *The Well-Played Game* and *The New Games Book* and understood that the games I played in grade school were made with a specific intention. Perhaps this is why, while reading *The Well-Played Game*, I didn't need any convincing when it came to the ideas it presented. It even felt like what was written there was what I had believed about games and play all along but never had the words to communicate. Probably due to the fact that I was able to play so many New Games at a young age, the thinking behind them seemed to just completely and intuitively make sense.

Now I find myself creating games and media for theme parks where we want our guests to have a positive experience that is also the best experience possible. This means we want them to walk away from their play experience feeling like the hero. Because of this I always find myself tapping into the lessons I learned from *The Well-Played Game*, in that I try my best to move out of the player's way as a designer. I try not to let the systems of the game hinder the player's experience but instead facilitate it. At times this means players cannot lose, but in the context of theme parks this seems to fit quite well with Bernie's philosophy of play.

My hope is that, just as I was exposed to Bernie's philosophy at a young age through the games we played during PE, I can play the role of introducing this philosophy to the next generation as they enjoy games within theme parks.

BEING IN THE WORLD

In this last chapter of the book, I want to talk about the role imagination can play in our relationships with each other and the world. How it can give us a way to talk about our role within the world, like in *The Label Game* where we wear nametags that tell the world how to see us, at least for the next five minutes. How it can help us to interpret the world and be in it. How it can even help us change and make and remake the world.

Imagination isn't a way of hiding from the world. It's a magical and powerful way of being in the world, of seeing and responding and interacting and changing and existing and coexisting.

IMAGINATION'S ROLE IN CREATING THE WORLD

Sometimes I like to look out at the world and pretend everything is playing.

I pretend that the trees are, in their own long, slow time, stretching, dancing, and waving at each other. And the clouds are sometimes somersaulting, sometimes rolling downwind, and sometimes dressing themselves up as things and beings. And the flowers are silently singing songs of color, one word a day, their music written in notes of perfume. And the birds are, you know, delighting in flight. And the squirrels are playing tag. And the breeze is seeming to come out of nowhere and suddenly caressing your cheek as if to say "peek-a-boo." And the rocks and pebbles are playing dead. And the rest of us are playing some kind of hide and seek, perhaps, waiting to be found.

And when I pretend like this maybe I notice things that I wouldn't otherwise have noticed, or I feel present in the world in a way that I wouldn't otherwise feel present, or I share my pretendings with someone else and add those pretendings to their own pretendings and suddenly we're in the world *together* instead of just being in the world next to each other. It transforms everything. It is wonderful.

Imagining the world, and imagining *in* the world, feels like the greatest gift we have. And although it happens in our imaginations, the things we imagine can expand from there into the world itself.

The things we imagine can *become* the world.

Yuval Noah Harari writes in his 2011 book *Sapiens: A Brief History of Humankind*:

> Over the centuries, we have constructed, on top of this objective reality, a second layer of fictional reality—a reality made of fictional entities: like nations, like God, like money, like corporations. As history unfolded, this fictional reality became more and more powerful, so that today the most powerful forces in the world are these fictional entities. The very survival of rivers and trees and elephants depends on the decision of fictional entities like the United States, like Google, like the World Bank. Entities that exist only in our imagination.

I hope this quotation is enough to get you interested in more from Harari. I find his thoughts on the evolutionary power of the collective imagination both brilliant and chilling. The notion that "fictional reality" has more power over our lives and our planet than physical reality is almost too huge to grasp.

Here's one more quote from the book:

> Sapiens rule the world, because we are the only animal that can cooperate flexibly in large numbers. We can create mass cooperation networks, in which thousands and millions of complete strangers work together towards common goals. One-on-one, even ten-on-ten, we humans are embarrassingly similar to chimpanzees. Any attempt to understand our unique role in the world by studying our brains, our bodies, or our family relations, is doomed to failure. The real difference between us and chimpanzees is the mysterious glue that enables millions of humans to cooperate effectively.
>
> This mysterious glue is made of stories, not genes. We cooperate effectively with strangers because we believe in things like gods, nations, money and human rights. Yet none of these things exists outside the stories that people invent and tell one another.

Imagination is not just in the world, and of the world. It helps us to make the world.

We'll come back to this idea in a minute. But first, the last of the four *Blather* games in this book.

SOMETHING TO PLAY: *THE BLATHER CHORALE*

There's another version of *Singing Blather* in which you focus your stream of consciousness into a conceptual spillway. It is based on a very funny, often silly, and oddly healing movement called "Complaints Choirs." Wikipedia explains a Complaints Choir as "a community art project that invites people to sing about their complaints in a choir together with fellow complainers." *The Blather Chorale* is similar in affect, but far less artful.

Our purpose:

- To make an activity that's a bit like Complaints Choir but that people could do instantly, spontaneously, without any preparation
- To help people express whatever it is they need to express, even though it's just as likely that nobody hears them
- To build community
- To help people have fun
- To make people laugh

One person is the conductor. Everyone else stands in a choir-like array. When the conductor signals, everyone starts singing their complaints about whatever they feel like complaining about. They are all singing to the same tune. My favorite for this is the "Ode to Joy" from Beethoven's Ninth.

What do you complain about? Well, whatever you feel like complaining about!

- "My hairdryer broke and now my hair has dried a funny shape . . ."
- "I feel weird about this singing and I don't know what to say . . ."
- "I would like to quit my job but don't know what else I could do . . ."
- "Bom bom bom bom something something, anyway my ankle hurts . . ."

The conductor can get as conductor-like as they so desire, getting the choir to sing more loudly or more quietly, appointing people to be soloists or to sing duets, and so on.

Singers can choose to sing whatever words in whatever languages compel them, or in complete gibberish. No rhymes or reason, either, are required.

Complaining noises are also encouraged. Oy!

In this way, we can take *Blather*—the game we can play in so many ways—and use it as a way to think and talk and sing about the world, to each other.

THE ECOLOGICAL IMAGINATION

One of the ways that imagination can help us to be in the world is through what I like to call the *ecological imagination*. In her blogpost on the topic, landscape artist Paola Fiorelle Berthoin describes it thusly:

> By living in one place for a long time, that place comes to live in me. Through the development of my senses, I tune into my surroundings of the garden and natural world at large, and physically through the water I drink and the foods I eat. I feel a dedication to protecting what I can, through active caring for the land and through expressing my imagination through creative endeavors. It is a relationship like any other; one that requires attention and integrity in action. These are all aspects I consider to be art and integral to my practice of creating.

Berthoin talks about "tun[ing] into" her garden and the natural world as an act of ecological imagination. It is, as she describes, an act of imagination that engages her creativity, that she experiences as a relationship, a physical act that requires her total presence, an act of "living in" and being lived in.

I love that term: "living in." It describes imagination not as some kind of intellectual pastime but as an act of immersion: of getting as far and as deep, physically and conceptually, into a particular moment in a particular place as you possibly can. It takes the whole idea of imagination deeper and further until it embraces the actual presence of your being in the world. Yes, that must be what the term "ecological imagination" means. Your imagination serving as the link between you and the environment in which you find yourself.

And once that link is strong enough, that's what you do, literally—find yourself.

We must, to understand a concept like ecological imagination, reimagine imagination itself. We must think of imagination as located not just in our thoughts but in our bodies as well—our bodies entire. We hear a bird song, and we turn to it, turn to look, turn to listen. We make our bodies still. We ourselves become silent. We pass a bakery, and we smell the bread. We slow down. Still our other thoughts. Breathe in. Imagining the bread into being. And we catch a glimpse of a reflection that we imagine to be ours. And we hear sounds that we imagine to be produced by cars. We sense the presence of what we imagine to be a crowd of people walking along the street with us. We can almost taste what we imagine to be the taste of bread. Rye? Probably pumpernickel.

SOMETHING TO PLAY: *WAYS OF BEE-ING*

Just like with any other type of imagination, we can train our ecological imagination—and have fun doing it. We don't necessarily need anyone else to be around to do this. But we do need the world. And we need to pay attention to it. And then we can play in our imagination and between our imagination and the world.

Let's say it's an unusually beautiful day, and you and everyone with you are one in it—separately together.

You find yourself watching a bee. Or maybe the bee found you. And you're just watching it do its bee thing. You know, flying from flower to flower, packing pollen onto its legs, all abuzz.

And (you guess because of this imagination thing you've been toying with so intensely of late) you decide, for the fun of it, to try to imagine what it is that the bee is seeing, sensing, feeling. It isn't hard. It's fun.

You find you can use your imagination to connect you. You can go from seeing the bee to being the bee. And you, as the bee, see more clearly, more details, feeling what the leaf feels like on your many feet, what the flower looks like through your multifaceted eyes, how your wings feel when you stop flying, the weight of the pollen ball on your leg, how the flower stem flexes from your weight.

Feeling the warmth on your back, tasting the light breeze for the scent of sugar, springing off into the wind, somehow knowing that your sisters are around, close, all of you seeking sweetness.

Can they lead you somewhere sweeter?

You, landing on another stem, the stem bending, bouncing under your weight. You, touching the soft petals with your front legs, your eyes alight in the bright yellow. Tasting, harvesting, springing off into the air in search of yet more sweet delight.

Would you rather see the bee, or be the bee?

Both, you answer. Both.

THE COMPASSIONATE IMAGINATION

In her 2016 NPR interview, popular Australian TV star Marta Dusseldorp comments:

> I think storytelling is important for maintaining cultural integrity, identity. I think identity leads to compassion, and compassion and imagination go hand in hand. And I think if you have an imagination, then you can understand how people who are less fortunate than you need your help and you can reach out to them. And I love connecting with the—especially in live theater—you connect with people. And to me, that's the most satisfying experience I've ever had in my life—is when I talk to people and I enrich their lives. I give them a chance to reflect on themselves, on who they are and their parents and their grandparents and their children. And that's what I'm here for—on the earth—is to be a human being with other human beings.

This insight about the connection between imagination and compassion underscores that this is yet another gift that imagination brings us. Imagination connects us, and offers us the ability to connect compassionately. It helps us understand and relate to other people's lives and loves, regardless of social strata, ethnic inheritances, physical or mental abilities. It is sharpened by our exposure to good literature and theater, television and film, through the best of our arts and artists. It is a gift that restores to us the best of our humanity.

It is best received by those whose imagination is highly developed, who delight in what their imagination brings them the way we delight in each other when we rediscover each other in play.

Imagine that.

Is it possible, I ask myself, that the compassionate imagination is not simply intellectual? Isn't it physical, too? Isn't it not only physical but emotional, as well? We don't just think it. We don't just imagine it. We feel it. Isn't it not just physical, intellectual, and emotional but social? It connects us to each other. Isn't it planetary? Doesn't it connect us to the world? Isn't it an attribute of existence itself?

As the UC Berkeley's *Greater Good* project states:

Compassion literally means "to suffer together." Among emotion researchers, it is defined as the feeling that arises when you are confronted with another's suffering and feel motivated to relieve that suffering.

Compassion is not the same as empathy or altruism, though the concepts are related. While empathy refers more generally to our ability to take the perspective of and feel the emotions of another person, compassion is when those feelings and thoughts include the desire to help. Altruism, in turn, is the kind, selfless behavior often prompted by feelings of compassion, though one can feel compassion without acting on it, and altruism isn't always motivated by compassion.

While cynics may dismiss compassion as touchy-feely or irrational, scientists have started to map the biological basis of compassion, suggesting its deep evolutionary purpose. This research has shown that when we feel compassion, our heart rate slows down, we secrete the "bonding hormone" oxytocin, and regions of the brain linked to empathy, caregiving, and feelings of pleasure light up, which often results in our wanting to approach and care for other people.

It seems to me that compassion is not only an act of imagination but also another kind of imagination itself: an imagination that is not only part of the way we think but also part of the way we sense, the way we experience the other. When we feel compassion, we connect emotionally, we connect viscerally. We suffer the suffering. We feel it—mind, body, and soul.

The connection between compassion and imagination is also a connection between imagination and the human being.

Daniel Goleman, the "emotional intelligence" guy, says this in his 2007 TED Talk:

> There's a new field in brain science, social neuroscience. This studies the circuitry in two people's brains that activates while they interact. And the new thinking about compassion from social neuroscience is that our default wiring is to help. That is to say, if we attend to the other person, we automatically empathize, we automatically feel with them. There are these newly identified neurons, mirror neurons, that act like a neuro Wi-Fi, activating in our brain exactly the areas activated in theirs. We feel "with" automatically. And if that person is in need, if that person is suffering, we're automatically prepared to help.
>
> At least that's the argument.
>
> But then the question is: Why don't we? And I think this speaks to a spectrum that goes from complete self-absorption, to noticing, to empathy and to compassion. And the simple fact is, if we are focused on ourselves, if we're preoccupied, as we so often are throughout the day, we don't really fully notice the other.

So compassion—this feeling that allows us to connect so intimately with other beings, this ability to imagine someone else's suffering so deeply that we sense their pain, that their pain hurts us, too—is the play mind connecting us to ourselves, our humanity, and the world.

When we exercise our ability to be compassionate, we connect to life. We imagine that we can feel this animal is in pain, we are moved by the beauty we imagine in the sunset, we are stirred by the anger we imagine to be rampant in this crowd, this nation. We grow dizzy imagining how deeply out of balance our weather has become. Our compassionate imagination leads to becoming at one with the totality of existence, totally.

SOMETHING TO PLAY: *THERE MUST BE A GOOD REASON*

So, here's a little exercise.

You decide on something you think is rude or just plain wrong, and you take turns coming up with good reasons for people to be behaving that way. Someone starts: "Did you hear that guy honking his horn over and over?" And then you take turns building a better and better reason for his behavior:

- "Maybe he's on his way to see his wife in the hospital . . ."
- ". . . and she just had a baby . . ."
- ". . . and she forgot what name they decided to call it . . ."
- ". . . and he's lost . . ."
- ". . . and running low on gas . . ."
- ". . . and his wife forgot her cellphone . . ."
- ". . . and the hospital called to say she keeps on asking for him . . ."
- ". . . and he has to go to the bathroom . . ."

It's fun. It's the kind of game you can play with the family, in the car, or at a restaurant, or in the supermarket, or in line.

And it kind of lightens things up, even though maybe those people really are bastards.

You can add to one excuse, or you can all try to come up with different excuses and then think about which one is the best—either way.

My wife taught this game to me. She likes to play it with herself when she's driving or in some place that's crowded. Whenever someone does something rude, like cut in front of her, she tries to think of an explanation for that person's behavior. Not a condemnation. An exercise in compassion.

As it happens, my son and his beautiful family live in a place called Moshav Mevo Modi'im, a small community near the Israeli town of Modi'in that was started by friends of the great Jewish spiritual singer and sage Shlomo Carlebach. While visiting them, we were invited to the home of Ben Zion Solomon, one of the founders of the settlement, who plays in a band called BenZion Solomon and Sons (and I mean *plays*). Dina, his wife, happened to mention that she played a game like this with her kids. She explained that it was an important part of her spiritual tradition to practice this kind of thinking. A spiritual discipline. In Hebrew, it's called *dan l'kaf z'chut*, or "the benefit of the doubt." And we thought it was just a game.

THE MORAL IMAGINATION

Life gets complicated. And so do we. So complicated that we sometimes get lost in the fold. It seems our moral compass has lost its poles. We do things that are wrong. We wrong people. We wrong ourselves.

Morality is another one of those intangible things about the world and about us. Another sensibility that relies on our imagination, on our connection to the play mind—our ability to imagine the consequences of our behavior, how it will be received, how it will impact others, how it will affect their relationships to themselves, to others, how it will affect their ability to make sound moral judgments.

There's a term coined by Edmund Burke in his 1790 essay *Reflections on the Revolution in France* that I, as an eager student of everything imaginary, find myself having to share with you. The term: "moral imagination." Burke wrote of it when speaking of life during the French revolution:

> All the pleasing illusions which made power gentle and obedience liberal, which harmonized the different shades of life, and which, by a bland assimilation, incorporated into politics the sentiments which beautify and soften private society, are to be dissolved by this new conquering empire of light and reason. All the decent drapery of life is to be rudely torn off. All the super-added ideas, furnished from the wardrobe of a moral imagination, which the heart owns and the understanding ratifies as necessary to cover the defects of our naked, shivering nature, and to raise it to dignity in our own estimation, are to be exploded as a ridiculous, absurd, and antiquated fashion.

Not a very happy view of things, perhaps. But, then again, the French Revolution was, for most, not a very happy time.

But for students of the imagination, it's a revelatory connection. The implication that our moral sense, our ability to pursue a moral life, is contingent on our ability to imagine what a moral life might be and how we might pursue it—this is yet another insight into the power of imagination and its impact on our human being.

In her summary of John Paul Lederach's 2005 book *The Moral Imagination: The Art and Soul of Building Peace*, Michelle Maiese shares a succinct and extremely useful definition of the concept: the moral imagination is "the capacity to recognize turning points and possibilities in order to venture down unknown paths and create what does not yet exist."

What is uniquely powerful about Lederach's approach is how aptly he applies that term to the art of building peace. Maiese writes:

> the moral imagination is the capacity to imagine and generate constructive processes that are rooted in the day-to-day challenges of violence and yet transcend these destructive patterns. In Lederach's view, the moments of possibility that pave the way for constructive change processes do not emerge through the rote application of a set of techniques or strategies, but rather arise out of something that approximates an artistic process. Lederach maintains that the art and soul of social change should inform peacebuilding efforts. Lederach's methodology and writing style throughout this book reflect his emphasis on art and imagination. His inquiry is not linear or strictly analytical, and he repeatedly appeals to imagery, metaphors, and stories to spark readers' imagination.

In describing Lederach's understanding of the role of imagination and creativity in building peace, Maiese writes about the transformative power of creativity, the way it can move us, the way it can remind us of our shared humanity. And she writes about the implications for us outside the artistic contexts that we normally associate with creative acts:

There is something transcendent that takes place both in artistic endeavors and in authentic reconciliation. Like artistic processes, reconciliation is not linear. It proceeds in all kinds of unexpected ways, has its own sense of time, and is not chronological. Like a creative endeavor, reconciliation has its own inner timing and cannot be forced. It arises from the heart as much as from the head and is most effective when it expresses a message that is simple and honest. The knack for play and for seeing the life inside of things is highly important. Lederach recommends that peacebuilders begin to see themselves as artists who feel a sense of connection to what they create, love for what they do, and a desire to bring beauty to what they build. The work of peacebuilding and social change needs to move beyond analytical techniques and tap into people's more artistic selves.

So, now, to the ideas of the creative imagination, the ecological imagination, and the compassionate imagination, we can add the moral imagination—all of which together help us begin to appreciate the apparently infinite reach of the playground of the imagination.

HAVING FUN TOGETHER

It's occurred to me, reading these works about creativity, or about imagination and compassion, or about imagination and ecology, that I know exactly the place, the structure, the experience, the phenomenon that leads to the development of the empathic potential. Yup.

It's what we call "having fun together." Because when we play together—especially when we play primarily for laughs, for the sheer fun of experiencing the combined excellence of being together, free together, of being our own officials, our own referees, makers and interpreters of our own rules—what maintains us in the sheer joy of it all is empathy.

When someone gets hurt, we stop the game. When someone, especially when several of us, even more especially when we all do something spectacular, we cheer, laugh, our neurons dancing together in the sheerness of shared glee. When we play together like this, freely, spontaneously, your play ignites mine, your pleasure, your funniness, your humanness kindles in me mine. Yes, playing together we build the connection, the community, the grounds of empathy.

All these things we've been reading about, extolling free, open play—all those authors who are attempting to share with us not only the miracle but the fundamental need for playing like this together—yes, I think that, more than in any other sphere of our collective endeavors, in playing together, for the fun of it, we learn empathy, we develop empathy, we teach empathy.

Which brings me to a very little, simple game—a much littler game than we might expect from something as weighty as a discussion of the moral imagination.

SOMETHING TO PLAY: *PASSING HUMANITY*

Since this game is played in the real world, the imaginary part is what happens when someone looks you in the eyes.

One of my favorite things to do when I go for a walk is to make passing contact with strangers. It's a fine art, requiring careful timing and sophisticated strategy.

A pass begins anywhere between ten and five paces (the fewer the paces, the greater the challenge) from the stranger. During this time, you must establish eye contact and determine the form of encounter, verbal or non. Each has its own range. Nonverbal can vary from smile to wave to hat-doffing (for the hatted few). Verbal can vary from "hi" to "hello" to "howya doin" to "beautiful day" and beyond.

It can be a very rewarding game, especially when someone actually acknowledges and returns your greeting, the degree of reward depending on the form that response takes relative to your opening play. So, for example, a smile and a nod in response to your opening smile is significantly more rewarding than a nod or smile alone. A verbal response to your nonverbal opening is even more rewarding. Clearly the combinations are endless.

It can be an equally disheartening experience when your gambit of greeting is not returned.

To bridge the psychic abyss left by a Gambit Declined, I, from time to time, like to keep score. Every time I get a response, I give anywhere from one to ten points to Humanity. In like manner, when I don't get a response, I chalk it up to Man's Inhumanity to Man. Since I am on the side of Humanity, I am always gladdened when Humanity wins. Consequently, I am constantly exploring new and more effective strategies to secure Humanity's ascendance in the Great Game. And when the victory goes to the dark side, I, at least, am not personally implicated.

One of the things that makes this game so richly playworthy is all the variables. The allure of finding a winning strategy often keeps me smiling and waving even when Humanity is ten or even twenty points behind.

It is in this spirit that I reveal one of my most exemplary and successful strategies.

First, you need to find someone with a baby. I do like babies, by the way, so the following is no mere ploy. The trick is to smile at the baby first. Not that you'd expect to get a smile back. Depending on how many paces you are from them when you initiate the smile, you might go so far as to include a mini, baby-appropriate wave. The second and equally crucial part of the trick is to glance up from the baby in time so that the implied greeting is deflected upward to the adult. I've become so skilled with this strategy that Humanity has earned as much as eight points from a single passing encounter.

IMAGINATION AND ENDINGS

Even when we're imprisoned by our bodies or by society, we are still free to imagine. Anything. And the only thing standing in our way is our own unfamiliarity with our powers.

When we were children, we had no such obstacles to overcome. And now that we are adults, with so many more experiences, so much more knowledge to play with, we get too busy with other things, we lose our trust, our faith in our infinite abilities to dream whole worlds into being. It never goes away, our ability to imagine. But we neglect it. So we forget our own greatest freedom. We've let our imagination run fallow long enough.

But imagination isn't just a gift for the fun times.

You may remember, back when we were talking about *J'Accuse*, that game about dying, that I said a couple of things.

Dying isn't fun, I said. Being dead, in all likelihood, is not fun. Someone else's death, even a pet's death, is not fun. And yet, and yet playing dead is immensely fun. Fun of such immense immensity that we have managed to immortalize it in games like *Ring Around the Rosie*. And then, ashes is what we're on the way to becoming, ashes, ashes, and we all ultimately fall down. And, you know, laugh.

And there's playing dead. You know, just plain playing dead. And pretending to die, clutching at our throats and falling to the ground. And we grow, and still we need to play with death. There are, for further examples, countless vampire-themed games of death and resurrection. And *Mafia* and *Werewolf*. And so very many videogames, oh yes.

Like anything else we need to understand, especially when it comes to big, hurting things that are too big, too painful to grasp, death and dying are things we need to play with. Over and over again. Not because we need to understand them but because it's the only way we can even begin to accept them as real.

So we play. And we imagine. And then when the things that aren't fun happen for real, we still play and imagine.

We might imagine, for example, that the only reason birds sing is the sheer fun of singing, of having songs and the ability to give them voice. Or the fun of discovering themselves suddenly landing on a moving branch in a swaying tree in perfect balance. Or the fun of knowing that whenever the wind or whim takes them, they can take off, and fly.

Imagine that the only reason you laugh is because it's fun to laugh. Not because of the endorphins or the health benefits. Only because of the fun. Only because it's more fun than you can contain.

Imagine the same about squirrels scampering around and inside of trees, or bees buzzing, or flowers flowering.

Then every bird you hear, every squirrel or bee or flower you see, will be an invitation to have fun, too. To share the fun. To celebrate the fun.

Imagine we just assume that it's all for fun, all about fun.

WE, THE PRUI . . .
COLLEEN MACKLIN

My students and I made a very political street game in 2008 called *Re:Activism*. It involved teams running around New York City reenacting famous historic protests for points. Players imagined they were suffragettes in 1912, actively playing the part, chanting the chants, carrying "Votes for Women" placards. It wreaked playful havoc on city streets as passers-by did puzzled double takes, imagining they'd stumbled on some Rip Van Winkleian protesters marching for rights that had been granted long ago. A few intrepid pedestrians would even join in and imagine they were suffragettes, too.

Some years later, in 2012, I met Bernie at a festival for independent games called IndieCade. In his talk "A Conversation with Eric Zimmerman and Bernie DeKoven," he said something that's changed the way I make games. Even more, how I see the world. Bernie said, "Playing in public is a political act."

It hadn't occurred to me that plain old play—as a simple act of freedom—was political. I had been making political games in public. But this gamesome, wise man just announced that ALL play in public is political!

Mind. Blown. Forever.

Later that day, I found myself in a public park, eyes closed, groping for strangers, whispering, "prui?" I was hoping to find the elusive silent one. I kept on searching and searching until all went silent. The Prui had become everyone around me, welcoming me with giggles as I finally opened my eyes.

Prui is my favorite Bernie game—and on that day, he taught me how to play. Now, I teach my students *Prui*. It never fails to turn a class into a community (a "play community" in Bernie's words). We feel togetherness rarely these days, but when we do, it feels like finding and joining the Prui.

Fast-forward to today, to the women's marches, to protests in parks, at airports, on streets. Placards ranging from urgent seriousness to playfully witty. Playing? Some might say so, but most probably wouldn't—"it's not a game," they'd say. Demonstrating freedom in public? Yes—most would agree to that. Imagining? Indeed, a better future! In my mind, I would think, freedom + imagination = definitely playing—of the highest order.

Recently I had the opportunity to talk to Bernie about his book *The Well-Played Game*, which I'd been reading with my students. In it, Bernie says, "if you can't play it, change it." Such an exciting idea! If we can imagine a game together, we can change it, too. I asked him, was he thinking about democracy when he wrote that? That we can change the rules of the system if we decide to, together? And he said, "bingo."

Bernie's games teach us that when we're faced with rules that don't work for everyone, we can simply imagine new ones. We might appear to be alone, eyes closed, searching aimlessly. But if we just keep playing, we will find the Prui—and it will be everyone. Power to the players!

STEPPING ASIDE

JOHN SHARP

I have to admit, I was skeptical of Bernie at first. His ideas about play felt too loose, too subjective, and too touchy-feely for my punk rock sensibilities. They seemed to trivialize games at a time when we were struggling to get them taken more seriously as both an expressive form and as a subject of scholarship.

My skepticism melted away the first time I participated in one of Bernie's play sessions—at the 2011 Digital Games Research Association conference, where Bernie gave one of the keynotes. What stuck with me most, and what took me years to really understand, were Bernie's instructions for playing that afternoon. He treated each game, no matter how simple or silly, with great respect. He carefully taught us the rules, making sure everyone knew what we were going to do.

One of the first things he told us was that we were welcome to join a game when we felt like it, and if we didn't want to play anymore, that was okay, too—we could just stop. At the time, it felt arbitrary, pushing against the grain of my conception of games and gameplay—you don't just jump in and out of a game whenever you want. I came to realize the importance of that gentle reminder that we all have the power to stop playing. Bernie knew we weren't all ready to take on his radical approach to play, and so he gave us permission to step away when we weren't able or ready to see beyond our current circumstances.

In hindsight, I now see it took me nearly a decade to really understand Bernie's point, and to see the radical power of play. I eventually realized that Bernie puts play in front of game, with fun as the secret to making us all better people. I needed the permission to stop, if for no other reason than I wasn't yet really understanding what Bernie was teaching me. Bernie's games encourage us to think about ways we can interact with one another beyond the game, and beyond the social structures that confine us.

What if we could interact without hierarchy or competition? What would it take for us to be more playful in our everyday interactions? Wouldn't that be an improvement on the current state of affairs in almost every situation?

A LIGHTENING

TASSOS STEVENS

It is summer 2017, and I am driving to Indianapolis. I am going to spend time with Bernie, time talking about life and play and legacy, about making a game together—*A Game of Legacy*—as one small part of his infinite legacy. As I drive through the monotonic time of the freeway, I listen to a CD of Bernie, where he talks—no, Blue rhapsodizes!—about an imaginary playground. In this playground, I can imagine myself playing, playing with (another) myself, and then being witnessed by (yet another) myself, and so on, like I am dancing (with myself) in the infinite reflective space between two mirrors. This does more than pass that monotonic time. Inside me there is a lightening.

Later, in Indianapolis, we sit in the park near the De Koven house and talk about the game, watching kids play on the swings, which were themselves a bequest from Bernie. Walking back to his house, we are captivated by birdsong. And here begins another rhapsody of Blue, challenging me to think of the opposite of play—not work, not boredom, but . . . rigidity.

I imagine a framework built out of Meccano, my dad's favorite childhood toy. How if it is too rigidly fixed, then there can be no play in it, no possibility of movement—and you won't be able to play *with* it either, jokes Blue, present in my imagination as I write this. I think about how play is the infinite asking of what if . . . ? And how it is impossible if we are too rigidly fixed to what is. But also how the feeling of rigidity inside yourself when you grip too tightly onto something makes it impossible to play, to be playful of spirit. That lightening.

I write this under an inner sky heavy with grief, still bent out of shape, but gradually lightening. And the only thing to present in the face of this weight is a smile, a grin. So I smile as I remember Bernie and my dad, brilliant teachers both. And I imagine them each with another great love of their lives, ice cream. My dad with pistachio and chocolate gelato, gazing at the sky above Florence. Bernie with his root beer ice cream float at the other end of a Skype call.

I smile, and remember the blessings game—a game of out-blessing each other—that bobbed into our conversations in the Indianapolis summer. And the blessing Blue gave at the end of *A Game of Legacy* for all its imagined players to come: may all the games that you play in the future be as fun as you are today.

A LACK OF CONCLUSION

As you'll remember, all this delving into the nature of imagination was originally about fun. It struck me one day that of all the playgrounds I've visited, of all the places where I've found myself having real, deep, genuine fun, that place, the imagined one, is the one place connecting me to every place and every being my mind and body can reach. It is as much of an imagined place as it is real. It is the best of all possible playgrounds because it is always as real and as unreal as I need it to be.

Imagination is built on reality. It has a vast collection of loose parts—memories, experiences, myths, stories, teachings, songs, poetry, aphorisms, quotes, sayings, smells, pets, accidents, weather, adventures, lovers, glances, caresses, emotions—to assemble and reassemble, construct and deconstruct, building worlds beyond reason. Everything it encounters is another tool, another toy, another stage set, another theater, another playground, another game. Every game is imagination in action—a connection between self and other, the dance between, the play between.

And the reason for thinking so hard about all this? It is a gift of the play mind. A gift that you must first allow yourself to receive, then allow yourself to play with, then allow yourself to understand.

It's the infinite playground where you are endlessly at play. Where you are infinite. Where you finally get to play, entirely.

The observation that the play mind can be experienced even in the most structured of pursuits first made itself known to me forty years ago, when I was writing *The Well-Played Game*.

All play can transcend its finitude at any moment, leaping out of finite time and body to embrace the totality.

The excitement that kept me writing came from the discovery that I wasn't really writing just about games and play. Every time I put the practices of play into words, I experienced a kind of resonance with something that penetrated much deeper—into society and morality, community and culture, art and religion, politics and human nature. I'd describe an experience I had playing ping-pong with a friend and find that I was writing about an experience of communion with the divine. And I think everyone who designs or dreams about games, about bringing people into play, is similarly compelled by these levels of meaning.

To make rules is to delineate freedom; to invite play is to invite the human spirit. It is this resonance that makes all my work so deeply fun. It is what keeps me writing and teaching and speaking and exploring and inventing new ways to play.

I didn't fully realize what my play/work was all about until several decades after the publication of *The Well-Played Game*, when computers had become ubiquitous, and excerpts from the book were making their way into textbooks for students of game design. A few years after that, I began being invited to speak at game conferences in Europe and the United States, and I discovered that my core contribution to this new world of game design was the rather simplistic observation that "it's easier to change the game than the players."

To find the rules that can keep us all in play—all of me, all of you, all of us. And then to play completely, without limit.

Sure, you could play for points. Sure, you could practice and exercise until you could get more points than almost anyone. And just as sure, you could play a game that was basically pointless, without referees, or score, or goal even—just and only for fun. I came to realize that the most important function of games is to make it more possible for people to play together, to become infinite, together. Rules are tools, guidelines, and nothing more.

And it took me another decade to acknowledge that we don't even need games to have the experience that I now know as "infinite play." That it is the core experience in all arts, in all pursuits of knowledge and mastery, justice and freedom: to find the rules that can keep us all in play—all of me, all of you, all of us. And then to play completely, without limit. To become unimaginable.

"Everything you can imagine is real," writes Picasso.

"As long as you continue imagining it to be," comments De Koven.

QUITTING IS HEAVENLY
ELYON DE KOVEN

We all know the number *one*. Yet you'll never meet *one*. We use it all the time, but it's all in our mind, a shared game.

Not to say one is an imaginary number. Well, it is, but it's a boring one. *i* is more interesting. *i* is zero ones plus one *i*. Imaginary numbers are two-dimensional. They are at least as real as real numbers. In fact, only with imaginary numbers could we reach the moon.

We can reach even further. As the Story goes, everything we feel, we do, we make, everything we know as fact—that all took six days to create. Like the six sides of a die, a whole complete toy. But on the seventh, the Game Maker cheated, quit playing . . . and behold it was Good. A new Game was created: Not-Playing. A Game beyond the six, beyond the senses, beyond merely playing; this divine Quitting posited a perspective of playing-with, playfulness, fullness, being. So deep, this fun, this imaginary Sabbatical life, this two-step playing in concert with the real.

We can play a game we all know, like marbles or thumb wrestling, and then we can imagine a new way to play; we can allow ourselves and each other to cheat or quit, nobody the Loser or even Losing, rather simply leaving the "real" game and entering a new one. Playfulness is like playing imaginary games, it's like imaginary numbers: it gives us more play space, it extends our playground. Playfulness allows our imagination to play too, helping us be even more One than one can be by oneself. Playfulness can get us to Heaven.

Wanna play a game?

AFTERWORD

ERIC ZIMMERMAN

As Holly and Celia and I were finishing this book, editing the very final (and very overdue) manuscript draft, I was also attending a conference on games in Berlin. I was explaining this project—this book you are now reading—to someone who wasn't familiar at all with Bernie De Koven.

So I found myself trying to describe Bernie: his work, his ideas, who he was, what he did. I found myself, surprisingly or unsurprisingly, struggling for the right words.

I said something like:

Bernie De Koven . . . was a game designer, but not a commercial kind of designer.
He was an educator, but not like a classroom teacher.
Bernie wrote books about play, but they're not academic analyses or books of rules.
He was an advocate and an activist—but he didn't protest or make policy—at least not in the way you might think.

This was proving more difficult than I had anticipated. I pressed on:

He played games, and taught others to play . . .
He was a friend, and a colleague . . .
Bernie was kind of like a shaman . . . or maybe more like the shticky Jewish uncle you always wished you had . . .

At a certain point I gave up. I had never before been asked to put the essence of Bernie into words. So I had never been forced to realize just how impossible the man was to summarize.

Maybe I managed to describe him. Maybe not. Maybe after finishing this book, you can understand what I was trying to say.

For those of us who knew him, Bernie simply *was*. Like Tuesdays. Or sunshine.

He was deeply playful and utterly accessible, always available for a chat or an email or a hug. I walked away from every single encounter with Bernie glowing with happiness, somehow feeling more rooted in my own self.

Which is why it has been so hard to imagine a world without him. Bernie passed as we were working on this book. His life and his death mark moments on either side of this project.

Only now, as we reach the end of this process, have I realized that putting this book together has perhaps been our way of reconciling his absence from the world.

And yet—this book is also the exact opposite of marking a loss. It is also our attempt to call him into being, to imagine him and make him real. We sing a song of Bernie. Bernie Blue De Koven.

The song continues. And a one, and a two . . .

* * *

I want to thank everyone who played a part in this rag-tag orchestra:

The absolutely spectacular Holly Gramazio, who magically stitched together this book from countless fragments into a powerful whole. Celia Pearce, a relentlessly and reliably insightful coeditor. Doug Sery at the MIT Press, who never stopped trusting us with this highly unusual project. And all of the incredibly smart collaborators who shared their own reflections on Bernie for this book (Rocky, Jesper, Lee, Gonzalo, Sebastian,

Frank, Katie, Tracy, Adriaan, Greg, Ian, Zack, Stephen, Catherine, Mary, Doug, Akira, Colleen, John, Tassos, and Elyon).

Lastly, deep thanks to Bernie's indescribably lovely family who supported this effort and continue his spirit with epic Halloween extravaganzas and an annual Day of Play in Indianapolis.

Bernie, we miss you. Terribly.

In the meantime, we'll be here. Playing.

with love,
April 2019

Further Reading

The Infinite Playground draws inspiration from many different sources, both directly and indirectly. The list below includes a selection of Bernie's own writing, writings by the book's contributors, recommendations for further reading, and selected books from Bernie's personal library, as well as citations of works mentioned throughout.

SELECTED WRITINGS OF BERNARD DE KOVEN

Deep Fun, https://www.deepfun.com/. Bernie's blog. Includes articles and presentations by and interviews with Bernie in all media, as well as a comprehensive database of games.

Junkyard Sports: Make Sports Fun Again! (Human Kinetics, 2004). A collection of games played with discarded and recycled materials. Useful resource for those interested in putting Bernie's methods into practice.

A Playful Path (ETC Press, 2014). Musings on playfulness and the precursor in many ways to *The Infinite Playground*. Available in print-on-demand paperback through ETC Press/Lulu and as a free PDF.

The Well-Played Game: A Player's Philosophy (MIT Press, 2013). Bernie's classic text on play and games, originally published by Doubleday in 1978; reprinted by the MIT Press in 2013 with an introduction by Eric Zimmerman.

ADDITIONAL READING

The Association for the Study of Play (TASP). Organization of scholars who study physical play. It has published three peer-review journals: *Play & Culture* (1988–1992); *Play & Culture Studies* (1998–present), which replaced its conference proceedings; and *International Journal of Play* (2012–present). TASP was influential on Bernie's thinking, and he attended some of their conferences and collected some of their journals.

Children's Games in Street and Playground by Iona Archibald Opie and Peter Opie (Clarendon, 1969). A classic anthropological text that studies the practice and migration of regional folk games among British children.

Communities of Play: Emergent Behavior in Multiplayer Games and Virtual Worlds by Celia Pearce (MIT Press, 2009). In-depth ethnographic study of online game communities; it builds on Bernie's "play community" and "coliberation" concepts.

Critical Play by Mary Flanagan (MIT Press, 2009). A deep look into the subversive history of games, play, and art.

Deep Play by Diane Ackerman (Vintage Books, 1999). A consideration of play as a way of being in the moment and awakening creativity.

The Game Design Reader: A Rules of Play Anthology edited by Katie Salen and Eric Zimmerman (MIT Press, 2005). Collection of key readings in games studies; a great place to start if you are new to the field.

Game Design Workshop: A Playcentric Approach to Creating Innovative Games by Tracy Fullerton (Taylor & Francis, 2019). Foundational game design textbook.

Games, Design and Play: A Detailed Approach to Iterative Game Design by Colleen Macklin and John Sharp (Addison-Wesley, 2016). Contributors Sharp and Macklin's book on game design.

Games for Actors and Non-Actors by Augusto Boal (Routledge, 1992). A sourcebook for playful exercises and activities.

"The Hegemony of Play" by Ludica (Janine Fron, Tracy Fullerton, Jacquelyn Ford Morie, and Celia Pearce), in *Situated Play: Proceedings of the 2007 Digital Games Research Association Conference* (University of Tokyo, 2007). Focuses on the principle that players should control the game and not the other way around.

http://ludocity.org. A collection of street games and new sports.

ludology.org. Contributor Gonzalo Frasca's blog about game studies.

The New Games Book (Dolphin, 1976) and *More New Games* (Dolphin, 1981) by Andrew Fluegelman and the New Games Foundation. Foundational books on the New Games movement and wonderful sourcebooks for physical games to play with others.

Play and the Human Condition by Thomas Henrick (University of Illinois Press, 2015). An investigation of different ways of looking at play in order to understand its role.

Play Everything by Ian Bogost (Basic Books, 2016). A look at different ways of using play and its boundaries to change our experience of the everyday world.

Play Matters by Miguel Sicart (MIT Press, 2014). A discussion of play as a way of being in the world.

Playfulness: Its Relationship to Imagination and Creativity by J. Nina Lieberman (Academic Press, 1977).

Rules of Play: Game Design Fundamentals by Katie Salen and Eric Zimmerman (MIT Press, 2004). Game design textbook that introduced Bernie's work to the game studies community.

The Spiel. http://thespiel.net/. Podcast on games and play by contributor Stephen Conway. Conway has taken on Bernie's mantle of "Major Fun" and maintains his *Deep Fun* blog. At the time of this writing, Conway is also in progress on a documentary about Bernie.

The Study of Games by Elliott M. Avedon and Brian Sutton-Smith (John Wiley & Sons, 1971). Highly influential early book on children's play and games. Bernie was very influenced by Sutton-Smith and frequently attended the conferences of his Anthropological Association for the Study of Play.

"Sustainable Play: Towards a New Games Movement for the Digital Age" by Ludica (Janine Fron, Tracy Fullerton, Jacquelyn Ford Morie, and Celia Pearce), in *Proceedings of the Digital Arts and Culture 2005 Conference* (IT University of Copenhagen, 2005). Calls for a revival of the New Games movement.

Works of Game: On the Aesthetics of Games and Art by John Sharp (MIT Press, 2015). Contributor Sharp's book on the history and practice of games as art; it includes mention of Bernie's *Alien Garden* among the earliest examples of videogames created as fine art.

WORKS CITED

Berthoin, Paola Fiorelle. 2013. "Ecological Imagination." *Paola Fiorelle Berthoin* (blog). https://paolafiorelleberthoin.com/other1.

Boal, Augusto. 1992. *Games for Actors and Non-Actors.* Routledge.

Burke, Edmund. 1790. *Reflections on the Revolution in France, and on the Proceedings in Certain Societies in London Relative to That Event. In a Letter Intended to Have Been Sent to a Gentleman in Paris.* J. Dodsley.

Christensen, Jen. 2017. "Playful Humor: The Dalai Lama's Secret Weapon (and How It Can Be Yours, Too)." CNN. July 2, 2017. Updated July 10, 2017. https://edition.cnn.com/2017/02/07/health/dalai-lama-humor-how-you-can-have-it-too/index.html.

Csikszentmihalyi, Mihaly. 1990. *Flow: The Psychology of Optimal Experience.* Harper & Row.

De Koven, Bernard. 2014. *A Playful Path.* ETC Press.

De Koven, Bernard. (1978) 2013. *The Well-Played Game: A Player's Philosophy.* Doubleday. Reprint, with an introduction by Eric Zimmerman. MIT Press.

Dusseldorp, Marta. 2016. "Compassion and Imagination Go Hand in Hand." Interview by Scott Simon. *National Public Radio*, Weekend Edition, November 19, 2016.

Feynman, Richard. 1983. "Fun to Imagine." BBC Broadcast.

Giles, Harry Josephine. 2015. *Casual Games for Casual Hikers.* Self-published.

Goleman, Daniel. 2007. "Why Aren't We More Compassionate?" Posted December 2007. TED video, 13:10. https://www.ted.com/talks/daniel_goleman_why_aren_t_we_more_compassionate/up-next.

Harari, Yuval Noah. 2015. *Sapiens: A Brief History of Humankind.* Harper.

Hughes, Linda. 1983. "Beyond the Rules of the Game: Why Are Rooie Rules Nice?" In *The World of Play: Proceedings of the 7th Annual Meeting of the Association for the Anthropological Study of Play*, edited by Frank E. Manning. Leisure Press.

Litt, Eden. 2012. "*Knock, Knock.* Who's There? The Imagined Audience." *Journal of Broadcasting & Electronic Media* 56 (3): 330–345.

Lombrozo, Tania. 2016. "The Curse of the Inability to Imagine." *NPR Opinion.* June 20, 2016. https://www.npr.org/sections/13.7/2016/06/20/482756327/the -curse-of-ignorance-and-the-curse-of-knowledge.

Maiese, Michelle. 2016. "Summary of *The Moral Imagination: The Art and Soul of Building Peace* by John Paul Lederach." *Beyond Intractability.* June 18, 2016. https://www.beyondintractability.org/bksum/lederach-imagination.

Manu, Alexander, Chris Matthews, and David Dunne. 2006. *The Imagination Challenge: Strategic Foresight and Innovation in the Global Economy.* Peachpit Press.

Ono, Yoko. 1970. *Grapefruit.* 2nd ed. Simon & Schuster.

Pendleton-Jullian, Ann, and John Seely Brown. 2016. *Pragmatic Imagination.* Blurb.

Russell, Bill, and Taylor Branch. 1979. *Second Wind: The Memoirs of an Opinionated Man.* Ballantine Books.

Siegel, Dan. 2014. "The Self Is Not Defined by the Boundaries of Our Skin." *Dr. Dan Siegel* (blog). March 17, 2014. https://www.drdansiegel.com/blog/2014/ 03/17/the-self-is-not-defined-by-the-boundaries-of-skin/.

Smith, Phil. 2010. *Mythogeography: A Guide to Walking Sideways—Compiled from the diaries, manifestos, notes, prospectuses, records and everyday utopias of the Pedestrian Resistance.* Triarchy Press.

Thompson, Clive. 2012. "Clive Thompson on the Importance of Fan Fiction." *Wired.* May 8, 2012. https://www.wired.com/2012/05/st-thompson-fanfiction/.

UC Berkeley. 2019. "What Is Compassion?" *Greater Good Magazine.* https://greater good.berkeley.edu/topic/compassion/definition.

Vygotsky, Lev Semionovich. 2004. "Imagination and Creativity in Childhood." *Journal of Russian and East European Psychology* 42 (1): 7–97.

Weening, Hans. 1995. "Meeting the Spirit." The Religious Society of Friends. Revised 1997. http://quaker.org/legacy/charlestonwv/meeting-the-spirit.html.

"Why Science Needs Imagination and Beauty." 2013. BBC Future. November 27, 2013. https://www.bbc.com/future/article/20131127-secret-to-thinking-like-a -genius.

Contributors

Ian Bogost is a writer and award-winning game designer. He is Ivan Allen College Distinguished Chair in Media Studies and Professor of Interactive Computing at the Georgia Institute of Technology. Bogost is also a Founding Partner at Persuasive Games, an independent game studio, and a Contributing Editor at *The Atlantic*.

Stephen Conway is a writer, filmmaker, journalist, and game developer. He is the host of *The Spiel* and the man behind the Major Fun Award and The Spiel Foundation. He is currently editing a documentary on Bernie De Koven's life and philosophy of play.

Adriaan de Jongh is a game designer best known for the hit indie game *Hidden Folks*, a hand-drawn interactive searching game, and for experimental games like *Bounden* and *Fingle*, which move people out of the normal space of videogames by challenging players to dance, hold hands, and share physical interactions. He also has an awkward signature dance that he'll perform with every opportunity presented.

Elyon De Koven, PhD, son of Fun, husband of one, father of four, grew up surrounded by games, and continues to play as a programmer, scientist, and teacher.

Rocky De Koven. Artist, teacher, grandmother, and partner of the aforementioned illustrious and wise author. They shared humorous (and not-so-humorous) events and mini-moments for over fifty years. Their synergistic, playful mindset was key to a meaning-full relationship.

Mary Flanagan is an artist, designer, and author of several books including *Critical Play: Radical Game Design*. She is the founder of Tiltfactor, an R&D lab that uses its unique design methodology to incorporate fundamental human values and psychological principles to promote learning, attitude change, and behavior change through games and playful objects.

Gonzalo Frasca is Chief Design Officer at DragonBox, creator of a game-based, full-curriculum math learning solution now used in Finnish and Norwegian schools. He's also Professor of Videogames at Universidad ORT Uruguay.

Tracy Fullerton is an experimental game designer, professor, author, and founding director of the University of Southern California's Games program and Game Innovation Lab. Her games include the recently released *Walden, a game*, which was named "Game of the Year" at Games for Change 2017 and "Developer's Choice" at IndieCade 2017. Tracy is the author of *Game Design Workshop: A Play-centric Approach to Creating Innovative Games*.

Holly Gramazio is a game designer, writer, and curator with an interest in site-specific games. She founded Now Play This, a festival of experimental game design that runs at Somerset House as part of London Games Festival.

Catherine Herdlick is an award-winning designer, entrepreneur, artist, and educator who designs and evangelizes accessible, playful systems that make digital, physical, and hybrid spaces more meaningful, collaborative, and joyful. She is the Founder and Executive Director of the Come Out & Play Festival for street games and Associate Professor of Interaction Design at California College of the Arts.

Jesper Juul has worked in videogame research since 1998. An Associate Professor at the Royal Danish Academy of Fine Arts–School of Design, he has previously taught at MIT and New York University. He has published three books: *Half-Real, A Casual Revolution*, and *The Art of Failure*.

Frank Lantz is a New York–based game designer and Director of the NYU Game Center. He has created a number of award-winning games at his studio Area/Code, including the popular puzzle game *Drop7*. Frank's pioneering work on cross-media and real-world games has been widely influential and his writings on games, aesthetics, and culture have appeared in a variety of publications.

Colleen Macklin makes games and teaches at Parsons School of Design where she also codirects PETLab. She's a member of Local No. 12, creator of *The Metagame*. She coauthored *Games, Design and Play: A Detailed Approach to Iterative Game Design* and *Iterate: Ten Perspectives on Creativity and Failure*.

Celia Pearce is a game designer, artist, author, curator, teacher, and researcher specializing in multiplayer gaming and virtual worlds; independent, art, and alternative game genres; and games and gender. She is currently Associate Professor of Game Design at Northeastern University in Boston, and is the cofounder and Festival Chair of games festival IndieCade.

Sebastian Quack is an artist, game designer, and curator interested in play as part of the politics of urban society. Sebastian's work takes place in cooperative processes, with the Invisible Playground network, Drift Club, Playful Commons, Playpublik, and the Playsonic festival on music and play. He lives in Berlin.

Lee Rush is the founder of justCommunity, Inc., where he has served as Executive Director since the organization's inception in 1999. He held various positions as an administrator, counselor, and teacher in an alternative school and day-treatment setting from 1979 to 1986.

Katie Salen Tekinbaş is Professor in the Department of Informatics at the University of California at Irvine, a member of the Connected Learning Lab, and Chief Designer and cofounder of Connected Camps. Her work focuses on meeting kids where they are in order to design engaging, play-based experiences that transform youth futures.

John Sharp is a designer and Associate Professor at Parsons The New School for Design. He is the author of *Works of Game: On the Aesthetics of Games and Art*, and coauthor of *Games, Design and Play: A Detailed Approach to Iterative Game Design* with Colleen Macklin.

Tassos Stevens is Director of Coney and maker of all kinds of play–theater, adventures, and games–for people to take a meaningful part in. He visited Bernie in the summer of 2017 to make *A Game of Legacy* with him, in an exchange documented at www.alegacyofplay.net.

Akira Thompson is a game designer at RainBros and currently working with Universal Studios Japan on several unannounced projects. Previously, he produced the critically acclaimed game *Wattam* and was the head of community relations at IndieCade International Festival of Independent Games.

Greg Trefry loves to make physical and social games. He cofounded Gigantic Mechanic, a studio dedicated to making all manner of playful experiences. He also helps organize the annual Come Out & Play Festival.

Douglas Wilson is a co-owner of Die Gute Fabrik, a games studio based in Copenhagen, Denmark. He currently lives in Melbourne, Australia, where he is a lecturer at RMIT University.

Zack Wood is a game designer and visual artist from the US, now based in Japan. He discovered Bernie's work (and had the joyful opportunity to meet him) after moving to Berlin to explore games and play, and things were never the same. Play and playfulness inform all of Zack's work.

Eric Zimmerman designs play on and off the computer. He cofounded the New York City studio Gamelab, which is responsible for dozens of award-winning games including *Diner Dash*. He is a partner at Local No. 12, the design collective behind *The Metagame* and *Dear Reader*. Eric is the coauthor of *Rules of Play* and Professor at the NYU Game Center. Bernie continues to influence and inspire his work and ideas.